Patricia Mercier (Alloa) has written six books about mind-body-spirit and ancient civilizations. She is an artist, lecturer, the co-director of The Sun & Serpent Maya Mysteries School in the UK and Spain, and a focal point for healing and shamanic training. She has studied and travelled widely in the lands of the Maya in Central America. In 1995 she received a shamanic Solar Initiation and in 2000 she was initiated into the Sovereign Solar Order of Chichén Itzá (Mexico) by shamans and elders using quartz crystal skulls. This complements her experiences as a crystal healer and yoga teacher. She lives with her husband Mikhail in southern Spain and the UK.

By the same author

Maya Shamans – Travellers in Time
Secretos de los Chamanes Mayas
The Maya End Times – a Spiritual Adventure
Chakras
The Chakra Bible
The Chakra Experience (workbook and CD)

CRYSTAL SKULLS & THE ENIGMA OF TIME

A SPIRITUAL ADVENTURE INTO THE MAYAN WORLD OF PROPHECY AND DISCOVERY

PATRICIA MERCIER

WATKINS PUBLISHING

LONDON

This edition first published in the UK and USA 2011 by
Watkins Publishing, Sixth Floor, Castle House,
75–76 Wells Street, London W1T 3QH

1 3 5 7 9 10 8 6 4 2

Designed and typeset by Paul Saunders
Printed and bound by Imago in China
British Library Cataloguing-in-Publication Data Available
Library of Congress Cataloging-in-Publication Data Available

ISBN: 978-1-78028-005-9
www.watkinspublishing.co.uk

Distributed in the USA and Canada by Sterling Publishing Co., Inc.
387 Park Avenue South, New York, NY 10016-8810

For information about custom editions, special sales, premium and
corporate purchases, please contact Sterling Special Sales
Department at 800-805-5489 or specialsales@sterlingpub.com

Contents

List of Plates

1. Rare Tibetan crystal skull *Amar*, surrounded by twelve crystal skulls. From http://www.crystalskulls.com/gathering.html Photo © 2010 Lee Simmons, award-winning photographer and creator of the extraordinary 'Secret World of Crystals' oracle deck

2. *Amakua* and *Xamuk'u*. Photo © Star Johnsen-Moser

3. Rare Tibetan crystal skull *Amar*. Photo © crystalskulls.com

4. *AsKaRa*. Photo © M Baker, courtesy of *AsKaRa*'s guardians

5. Author and husband. Photo © M Baker

6. The Sun God Kinich Ahau breathing and speaking. Photo © M Baker

7. Ball-player's skull speaks within the ball as he achieves cosmic consciousness. Photo © M Baker

8. Vision serpent arising during ceremony. Photo © M Baker

9. *Compassion*. Photo © J Bennett

10. Early Maya carving of Sun God Kinich Ahau. Photo © M Baker

11. Hunbatz Men. Photo © M Baker

12. *Jomcata Mayab*. Photo © Lia Scallon

13. Red obsidian late-Neolithic shamanic tribal skull. Photo © LionFire

14. Crystal skull guardians presenting their skulls at a Maya initiatory ceremony. Photo © M Baker

15. Star Johnsen-Moser and *Xa-mu-k'u*. Photo © Alex Domingo

16. *Xa-mu-k'u*. Photo © Star Johnsen-Moser

17. The labyrinth – Temple 19, Yaxchilán, Mexico. Photo © M Baker

Introduction

I got up early and looked across the valley. Some 60km away the sea at Malaga was touched with a silver streak. In the distance, the smoky-grey Andalucian mountains formed a magical silhouette against a blazing orange ball of fire as Great Father Sun rose into a violet dawn sky.

Standing quietly watching, breathing in the essence of this spectacular sunrise quickly melting into rose-gold, the clouds twisted into the shape of a serpent undulating across the sky. Immediately other wisps of fine cloud gathered into the image of a skull just behind the serpent's head – an excellent portent! Today I was to speak to my publisher and, little was I to know this morning, this book was to be conceived.

'What is your fascination with crystal skulls?' people often ask me. Finding no immediate or rational answer to this question, I embarked upon a quest to find out. My deep experiences and traditional initiations with crystal skulls had begun in 1995 when Maya elders in Yucatán, Mexico, invited me to take part in ceremonies to manifest spiritual energies for the coming new age of the Maya, connected with the 2012 predictions and their calendars.

By handling and especially meditating with the skulls I underwent many transformations. I discovered that life-sized crystal skulls, particularly those carved from quartz, reveal to us the presence of a higher consciousness which, with focused intention, we can seek to embody in our own lives. Through what I learned I now believe the crystal skulls are a deep-memory trigger, urging us to use that consciousness in ways that animals cannot. Because of our place in species evolution, our development enables us to rise above both individual and immediate needs, to conceive a bigger picture of life.

Unlike other creatures, humans can study the past to learn from it. We can look forwards into the future to plan and make choices which affect all life-forms. We have the ability to give ourselves a better quality of life and, most importantly, leave something worthwhile for our children. This enables us to value the present moment, to appreciate our interactions with one another, with our wider environment and, along the way, it teaches us how to care for our planet.

I will always remember a little shiver passing down my spine as I heard the following Native American wisdom at a gathering of indigenous elders from the whole of the Americas. *It is vital that we cherish the Earth. We must leave her in a better way than we found her for the sake of our children, our grandchildren and our grandchildren's children, seven generations into the future.*

My journeys took me to wild and exotic places where I studied with wisdom-keepers and shamans. In ancient temples and the remote rainforest I received a number of initiations with crystal skulls and, as a practising crystal healer, I have come to understand the different vibrational qualities of crystals and stones. I have seen amazing jade skulls and other ancient artefacts recently discovered in the Himalayas between Tibet and China, and I have wondered at the huge pyramids in central China.

I asked Great Spirit – the words I use for God or Creative Intelligence – to show me connections between crystal skulls found in very different parts of the world, from Tibet to Mexico. Even in London, in a section of the British Museum, I gazed upon a stunningly clear quartz crystal skull said to have unusual properties, if rumours of its emission of sounds, light and movement are to be believed.

People seeing crystal skulls for the first time find them either spooky or fascinating – it's hardly surprising that few appear to be indifferent to them. Throughout the world are a number of collectors or, as they prefer to be called, *guardians* of crystal skulls. Occasionally, permission is given for their skulls to be handled by people with psychic abilities or to be placed upon a modern altar as a meditation focus. Sometimes these skulls are used as channels for spiritual, crystal or vibrational energy healing.

Crystal skulls, ancient and contemporary, are attracting a great deal of interest because of their apparent connection with the Maya people of Central America. I shall explain the reason for this as I take you with me on my colourful journeys to exotic places and inner realms. Along the way we will meet myth and magic and their companions on the flip side of the coin, history and science.

Imagine that you could look into the past or have the vision to navigate time future. It is not such an impossible idea since some of our ancestors believed that past and future are all around us in ever-expanding circles, and fully accessible within the present. Closely associated with Time are the images of skulls to be found in Central America, where real skulls are even gaily decorated for Day of the Dead celebrations. Death and regeneration, symbolized by the skull, is often accompanied by a 'vision serpent' of ancestral life-energy.

I have chosen to invoke myths within this story about my

quest that are primarily of rebirth, the future and co-creation. Imagine you are standing on the flat top of a towering stepped pyramid. Around you as far as you can see is a vast ocean of green vegetation. Occasionally a flock of bright yellow parakeets flits across the top of this tree canopy and a lone howler monkey begins its unearthly cries. As if synchronized by an unseen hand, conch shell trumpets sound out while clouds of fragrant copal tree-resin smoke billow around us.

A shaman-priest arrayed in a jaguar skin cloak and ceremonial headdress of quetzal-bird feathers steps forward. He is accompanied by a priestess carrying a sacred bundle that she carefully unwraps upon an ancient stone-carved altar, setting a mysterious smoky quartz crystal skull upon it. The shaman reverently lifts the skull up to acknowledge Great Father Sun, then walks towards you. This is your invitation to begin a quest with crystal skulls and look through them at worlds beyond worlds.

From the minutiae of cells to the vastness of space, everything is interrelated. What happens to one fragment affects all. But in addition let us look more closely, for the phenomenon of life, by its nature, needs to create a vehicle, a body to use, and it is morphogenesis, the dividing and structuring of growing cells, that builds the vehicle. When it is ready for ongoing sentient life, a living impulse enters in the form of light-encodements to begin the communication processes that spark between cells. This is just like building a house, but until it has life in it that house doesn't become a home. It needs a family and it needs a purpose – until then it is but an empty shell. In morphogenesis, cells join together into a pattern which, as it gains in complexity, evolves into more and more complex life-forms as the process itself evolves.

Science has now gone beyond Darwinian theories to explain evolution. The existence of crystal skulls causes us to confront within our own skulls the issue as to whether humankind has evolved as far as evolution can go.

However, at this pivotal point a higher creative intelligence exists with a plan for the positive advancement of life. Suppose this higher intelligence wanted to direct an impulse to strengthen the creative morphogenetic fields of life at a given time in our history. Where would this impulse be placed? Not, I suggest, in the minds of animals, that are unlikely to plan or evolve, but in humans. It would be placed into the seat of our consciousness, our minds, our skulls.

What better way to convey this message than with uniquely carved skulls, fashioned from a solid piece of sparkling crystal, to remind us of this? Skulls that would 'talk' or 'sing' directly to the consciousness inside our own heads; skulls that would emerge to coincide with humanity's development of silica-based technology – computers and complex instruments – to enhance brain power. The message would be embedded in a material that would survive intact over aeons of earth changes, a material such as stone or crystal – called 'frozen light' by the ancestors – and greatly valued for its beauty.

Some of the most stunning and powerful crystal skulls are carved from living, growing crystal called silicon dioxide, a very pure form of quartz, which is identical to that now artificially grown for use in microchips. Today we use these chips in computers for communication and a myriad of applications in the functioning of complex systems or machinery. We are even building intelligent computers that learn as they work. They replicate the morphogenesis of growing cells by self-selecting specific cells for specific purposes and then evolving that purpose into the next stage.

At this point in history we can pose two fundamental questions. Is it possible to concentrate our life-force sufficiently to further evolve our human species into a higher state of consciousness? Can we manifest a realization that evolution is no longer restricted to the three physical dimensions?

The answer to these questions fits like a key into our own skulls. My quest suggests we are the designated life-form which can turn that key, because we are the only fully conscious, upright, two-legged creatures on Earth. If we get it right we are promised a new rose-gold dawn. Indications from many quarters imply that, at the present time, we are standing, both watching and creating the dawn of super-intelligence. Such a dawning would not have been possible even 100 years ago, around the time when the first extraordinary crystal skull was found on an archaeological dig in present-day Belize by Anna Mitchell-Hedges.

It is this precise window in time which presents us with unimaginable challenges and incredible rewards. All the signs are positive, if we make the right choices, and if we heed the wisdom imparted to humanity by the Maya calendar-keepers of Central America, who maintain that we are presently within a 'Shift of the Ages'. The shift involves the fulfilment of ancient and archetypal myths on Day Zero of a calendar count of 5,125 years, part of a larger cycle of 25,920 years. (An introductory overview of the Mayan calendar, dates and day names is to be found in Appendix One.)

These myths speak of the return of *Ku-kul-kaan*, the Mayan name for Quetzalcoatl, the prototype enlightened human who, it is said, will return from the east on a raft of serpents. The symbolic promise embedded into human consciousness so long ago is that we can *all* create a higher life-form than that which currently lives on Earth. In consequence the development due to occur is a quantum leap forward into another type of evolution – let us call it 'spiritual' – not into 'God', our name for a deity, but into the actual mind-source fields of Creation.

Look deeper into the enigma of the crystal skulls and you will find they are here to remind us of something extraordinary, that they can take us into other-dimensional realities. Their subliminal messages demonstrate that we have a unique entranceway being shown to us beyond our five senses, beyond our extra-sensory perceptions, and the only requirement is to focus on a heartfelt intention to evolve thought processes within our own skulls. That is where the entranceway exists, and the key turns because therein lies the seat of consciousness.

Through my quest I found that we are very close to finding the truth. Yet this truth is laid before us not only on Earth but beyond this planet and beyond the stars. It is hidden in the culmination of ancient myth, lines of Time and archaic shamanic practices as well as in modern quantum theory.

The questions seem tantalizing. But the answers are simple and don't need complex calculations or scientific evidence. Crystal skulls are both a key and an answer. With their clarity we can unify consciousness deep within our own skulls. We become a focal point for the living consciousness-field that is all around us and for our internal consciousness. They then expand together at will, to connect with an extraordinary superconsciousness arena – which is the unity of consciousness – and is all One.

So enjoy my story and the adventures and the wisdom teachings it contains. But before you read on, close your eyes and, in the blackness, see a sparkling life-sized quartz crystal skull in a field of stars, and ask what it has to teach you.

·

CHAPTER ONE

The Cave of Skulls

The destiny of man is in his own soul.

– **HERODOTUS**, 'THE FATHER OF HISTORY', 494–23 BCE

Some things come back to haunt us – whether we are dead or alive.

Awakening from a long, long sleep, I look around the cave and call out two Mayan words, meaning 'jaguar star', the name of my quartz crystal skull: 'Balaam Ek, Balaam Ek!' Where is Balaam Ek, my beautiful and prophetic crystal skull, that I hid down here?

There's no answering voice. Just the silence of the grave – for there is nothing but human bones. A large quantity of them are arrayed around sparkling stone walls together with a dozen or so skulls, all turned to soft chalky stone by the constant drip of calcite-laden water.

It seems I'm trapped with these bony ancestors whether I like it or not, and it's going to be difficult to get out. I shift my position slightly, holding my head, which is pounding with pain and echoing with strange information.

Everything I saw, was it a dream? Did I explore the magical Maya ruins of Piedras Negras in the Guatemalan rainforest? Had the gunmen pursued us on the Rio Usumascinta as we sped away from the ruins in a motorboat? Did I really present the thirteenth crystal skull at a grail mass in the Heart of the Earth? Did I really take shelter in the cave at Tulum in Mexico, by the soft, warm Caribbean, as the Earth changes began and the sea churned into a tempestuous vision of hell?

Opening to Spirit

Slowly I recalled … I was no longer in Mexico. Only three or four hours ago, against all advice, I had ventured into this cave system alone. After that, something happened. I couldn't immediately recall what it was. I looked around again with the light from a match and found my head-torch. I was equipped with all the right gear and ropes, but I knew it was going to be a tight squeeze to clamber back to the surface, and my head was pounding. Despite wearing a hard hat, I realized I had somehow managed to knock myself out when I slipped and fell.

The cave is hidden high in the mountains of the Sierra in southern Spain, where my family frequently explored the rough terrain below the peaks. Always one for taking risks, I had now put myself in the position of contemplating the impermanence of life in this deep subterranean chamber, as I moved in and out of consciousness and vivid dreams.

Yet, awakening, I knew the ongoing story was waiting to be told, a story of how we are obsessed with death and skulls, holding as they do the essence of consciousness. I respectfully picked up one of the human skulls sitting in the dust alongside me. With the aid of my head-torch, with renewed interest I gazed around at other skulls of Neolithic 'ancestors' interred here. Some of them were of a strange, rather elongated shape. Why this was I didn't know.

My son had discovered the cave system some weeks previously. On that occasion we had walked a long way and thick grey banks of moisture-laden cloud were beginning to spin across the mountaintop, causing tiny wisps of pale numinous cloud to escape and scroll softly around the jagged rocks. Suddenly we found a hidden entrance, one we had not explored before, amongst yellow flowering gorse, rock roses and a tangle of prickly sprawling vegetation.

With the weather deteriorating we cautiously decided to leave, agreeing to return when the sun was shining. It's never a good idea to venture into caves when it's wet outside because of the risk of sudden underground torrents or rocks shifting. Exploration could wait for another day.

For now, all I knew was that I needed to clamber out of the cave, leave the ancestors' bones in their resting place and get back to the land of the living. With this accomplished, I started wondering about my fascination with skulls while I finally sat, dusty and tired, back in our house. As my husband Mikhail poured me a refreshing glass of deep red *vino tinto*, an old memory tried to surface.

My head was still pounding. The colour of the wine seemed to indicate blood, or a sacrament. Was it something mentioned in the Bible, something about Golgotha, 'the place of the skull', that was tantalizing me? I remembered that, as the Cross is to Christianity, the World Tree is the basis of Maya teachings from Central America, carrying many esoteric interpretations.

Taking another sip of the blood-red wine, I reflected on why people have a kind of morbid fascination with skulls. To many they are really scary. In a pile of ancient human bones, the skull is the most enduring part of the body. It has had magical properties attributed to it from time immemorial, being revered as a remnant of the soul of the ancestors, used as a drinking cup for dubious rituals and as an emblem for death and for secret societies. Beneath some old cities such as Paris and Naples, catacombs stretch for miles with thousands of skulls of former inhabitants interred in them.

Deep esoteric studies always seem to point in the same direction, suggesting that the skull is sacred because, in life, the head contains our brain, consciousness and even our soul. This is hardly surprising, for it is the location of the most evolved physiological energy in the human body, as well as the chakra energy centres of the 'third eye' and 'crown' in yogic systems. The chakras are foci of subtle vibrational energy developed in Indian esoteric practices, especially tantric yoga. It is now widely recognized that these two chakras are associated with sleep patterns and enhancing the ability to meditate.

Once over my shock and fall in the cave, a little voice inside my head emerged time and again, saying, 'The skulls have something to tell me.' So I decided to set aside a few hours to prepare and go into deep meditation, specifically focusing on the enigmatic skulls carved from crystal that had recently entered my life. I settled down to ask whether and how crystal skulls could bring a new spiritual dynamic into human consciousness.

My mind had focused on human consciousness before. I am involved in numerous aspects of healing, environmental and social affairs and so I reviewed the critical choices and challenges the human race is encountering. I highlighted areas of mental and physical changes, psycho-spiritual insights, environmental awareness, political and social changes leading to peaceful coexistence with all beings. Melding all this together, a holistic vision emerges that places a value on the interdependence of all life to co-create a balanced future.

Holding these reflective guidelines in my heart my process gradually deepened into meditation. I became aware I was being prompted by the crystal skulls to remember how we feel when in a divine loving situation, or when having a peak experience such as an enlightenment moment or a near-death experience. In these heightened states we can transmute our world. When truly 'in love' with someone there is no separation, only an enhanced superconsciousness that quickly merges into a consciousness of Oneness.

Eventually I returned to normal perceptions. I thanked all the skulls – the old human skulls from the cave and the crystal skulls that I knew about. Sometimes I began my meditations by looking at a photograph of one of the ancient crystal skulls. At the time I wasn't using a real crystal skull, so a photo gave me a deep connection to their essence. The crystal skulls seem to lead us from the everyday into the psycho-spiritual realms. Expect to be transformed! Earth 'guardianship' and personal energy-development go hand in hand and cannot be separated.

During quiet times I often remembered my very first experience with a special skull. It was carved from clear crystal, sitting shimmering in the centre of a circle of students at a crystal healing training in England some years earlier. Although much smaller than life-size and probably newly made in Brazil or Taiwan, it had a certain *presence*, and I came to understand that it was capable of being a transmitter of mysterious healing energies.

This crystal skull often 'spoke' to me and I even found that I could pick up something about its recent history. The crystal carver had put good intentions into making a skull from a specially chosen, unflawed block of rock crystal. This was important. It was carved with the love of his craft. Of course he had used power tools and grinders with diamond tips to do the laborious parts of the work, but each time he touched the crystal his intention was that of perfection and beauty in the object he was making. He encoded his thoughts and ideas into the emerging crystal skull as he worked. When finished, feeling pleased with his labours, he held the sparkling object up to the light to see its clarity and the inclusions in the crystal of a fine golden rutile mineral (dubbed 'angel hair') which shone like gold. He then set it upon a shelf with a number of others that he had created.

Once this crystal skull was purchased and in a new guardian's hands, it was treated to all sorts of beneficial rituals to wash, psychically cleanse and empower it to be a conductor of healing energy. It sat in the centre of the circle and radiated light to us all. Though it was a recently-made skull its presence was tangible and its potential untapped.

In some ways a contemporary crystal skull such as this is preferable to an old one since it is ready and waiting to be 'encoded' (programmed) with all manner of positive information. Exactly what this is depends upon how the healer wants to use it and what the crystal is able to communicate to them in a two-way contact. Often it's as though the crystal is simply waiting to be woken up to its true purpose – rather like the way we humans sometimes need to be prodded and prompted to wake up to our own true soul-purpose.

I learned many useful techniques during my crystal healer training, yet something within me remained unfulfilled. At that time, with pressures of work, I felt I was not allowing deeper mysteries into my life. It seemed as if the little sparkling crystal skull in the healing circle was prompting me to do something about this, and so I started to question what really inspired me.

One day I asked Mikhail, 'Why do I always seem to be attracted to crystal secrets and caves?' This was more a rhetorical question than a real question for him.

'Because you are a Scorpio, of course,' he replied. 'You can't help being drawn into mysteries – you can rise to great heights of understanding as an eagle, the alter-ego of a scorpion, or you can sink into exploration of the darker arts of magic.'

My stinging scorpionic tail began to rise with his assessment, but Mikhail, a Gemini, recognized this and began his flight before the sting could do its work. He continued, 'But you have an enquiring mind and want to know how and why the past can inform humanity's future. You want to learn more about subtle energies. I sense that you have a part to play in advancing human understanding of ancient crystal skulls.'

'Wow, that's a big statement!' I exclaimed. Little did I know what he meant, or what adventures and intrigue I would encounter as I set out to discover more.

Crystalline Questions

That night I remember drifting into a state of drowsiness, focusing my inner mind. I filled the cavity of my own skull with a crystalline frequency, visualizing it streaming in as liquid golden light. It flowed into all the little grooves and indentations in my mind so that it became like a shell of thin crystal within my head. It was a technique I was to employ on other occasions if I wanted to connect to crystal energy.

That same night I dreamt of a crystal skull. It shone with a golden light but inside it was a soft pink rose quartz colour, conveying a gentle feminine-like essence. I knew she had appeared in order to lead me on a quest. She would guide me as a 'spirit crystal skull' and perhaps one day I would even encounter her in the real world.

As my quest deepened, I found there were all kinds of crystal skulls, from miniature to larger than life-size ones. Some keepers of these skulls allow them to be used in meditation or to be held by people able to obtain information from them. Others only draw on them for healing, 'readings' or in ceremonies.

Meanwhile I established that crystal skulls are mainly associated with two continents – the Himalayan regions of Asia and the lands of the Maya people in Central America. Just a few that have been revealed to humanity today are classed as truly *ancient* – for example skulls which have acquired names such as *Mitchell-Hedges Skull of Love, Max, Sha Na Ra, Mahasamatman* and *Synergy.*

When examined with electron scanning microscopes and other modern technology ancient skulls are found to be entirely hand-carved and estimated to be over 1,500 years old. The problem with ascertaining the age of crystal skulls is that they cannot be carbon-dated like other artefacts such as pottery or bones. The source of the crystal can usually be established through scientific analysis by examining its properties and matrix structure, but the age of the carving simply does not reveal its secrets.

What *can* be ascertained is that numerous skulls were made using primitive techniques that left microscopic irregular groove cuts. They are regarded as 'old' when they are between 100 and 1,500 years of age. Examples are *Amar*, a skull from the Himalayas, the fine British Museum Skull and the Paris Skull. Finally, the classification 'contemporary' is given to new skulls carved in the last 100 years using modern tools such as electric rotary diamond saws. Nowadays quartz is even melted at high temperature and moulded into shape.

When microscopically examined, contemporary skulls have uniform miniscule grooves that easily identify the fact they were carved with power tools. Many contemporary crystal skulls are made of the finest pure rock crystal mined in Brazil, where detailed and skilful carving is done, whilst some are made in countries such as Germany and China.

Today skulls of diverse materials are readily available in many shapes and sizes. It is common to see clear quartz, amethyst, smoky quartz, yellow citrine or rose quartz as well as black obsidian, labradorite (a bluish stone with rainbows), jade of all colours and lesser-known minerals. Any mineral hard enough to take cutting and grinding without shattering has been carved into skulls in recent times. The ready availability of crystal skulls has somehow caught the imagination of the public. It seems not to be a random occurrence, since some unknown force is encoding new skulls with the information of our age, just as the older ones were encoded.

Crystal skulls pose many questions. I was to discover several complications during my quest. For example, skulls originating from the Himalayas and Tibet had a different historic fate to skulls from the Americas. For the most part they were lost for aeons in mountain caves or kept hidden away in monasteries. Their stories didn't pass into folklore like those from Mayan-speaking Central America. This is why so many people have been surprised that crystal skulls have been discovered in Tibet, Mongolia and China, seemingly well removed from the influences of the Mayalands.

This convinced me that there must have been connections between diverse peoples in the distant past. Historians theorize that, towards the end of the last Ice Age (about 10,000 BCE) people walked over a land bridge across the Bering Strait between Siberia and Alaska. According to this theory, these migrants eventually populated the whole of the American continent, North and South.

One day, Mikhail and I sat beneath the hot afternoon sun and chatted about this. 'Mikhail, I think that, in far-off times, there was more contact between civilizations than we give credit for today. Some Maya people still speak of their ancestors having lived in

Tibet and Atlantis whilst affirming, like other peoples, that the original impulse for life came from the stars.'

'Well, their wisdom-holders say that, following the Atlantean destruction, one group of survivors went north to become known as the Hopi, and another group remained in Central America to become the ancestors of the people there today. You remember how our Maya teachers, the *hau'k'in* Solar Priests, call four of their legendary founders of civilization "the Four Balaams", who came from the constellation of the Pleiades? They say they were the first interdimensional travellers to arrive on Earth.'

We had seen depictions of these beautiful interdimensional beings at Ek Balaam in Mexico, carved in stone. As if to indicate their god-like status, they stood there with wings and curiously elongated heads.

'Isn't it exciting?' I exclaimed. 'The same head shape is portrayed on Egyptian pharaohs, notably Akhenaten, as well as on Maya rulers and Andean mummies. Strangely, it is also like one or two of the skulls we found in the cave in Andalucía. It's popularly referred to as an extraterrestrial head since this shape does not fit into accepted morphology or the known development of humans.'

'A lot of people are sceptical about star travellers, forgotten civilizations and Atlantis ... ' Mikhail said, pouring me something to drink.

'I know, but I have strange dreams, even daydreams, where an odd collective memory keeps arising. These memories surface, it seems from nowhere, like the bubbles in this glass of soda, but now I nurture them with my research into myth and legend and absorb them with excitement.

'D'you know what I'm going to do? I'm going to seek out and ask crystal skull guardians what they know. I'm going to ask them to consult their crystal skulls, asking three simple questions, starting with something that really intrigues me about the fact that crystal skulls come from two continents.

'I want to ask them what the connection is between the ancient skulls from Central America and the Himalayas. Then I'll ask what the role of crystal skulls has been in the past and what their role is today, and finally I'll ask how the crystal skulls are connected with the evolution of spiritual consciousness.'

I thought the questions were simple, but the answers, like the nature of crystal itself, turned out to be highly complex and multifaceted.

·

CHAPTER TWO

Crystal Skull Initiations

The day science begins to show an interest in non-physical phenomena, it will advance more in a single decade than it has in all the centuries of its existence.

— **NIKOLA TESLA**, PHYSICIST

I began questioning some of the crystal skull guardians about the extraordinary information they were sharing with me, then my curiosity led me into an interesting encounter with a shamanic teacher in Britain. It involved intense secret ceremonies with crystals, resulting in my understanding some Egyptian past-life connections. During these encounters I held a large piece of double-terminated quartz crystal, with a natural point at each end. This particular crystal is also a 'timekeeper' and 'phantom', having multiple layers of growth within it which make up the shape of a pyramid pointing in two directions. This gives the holder the ability to travel forward or back in time. Perhaps my exploits were overseen by an ancient Egyptian God of Time, since *Horus* is the name that this crystal had acquired!

My esoteric studies then moved to the enigmatic indigenous Maya people of Central America. I became fascinated by their culture, whose deep mythic roots extend back to 'the time before time began'. Their traditional teachings have barely changed over the centuries.

Soon after encountering their complex system of calendars, my husband and I began keeping the day-count with the sacred *Tzolk'in* calendar, called *Chol q'ij* in Guatemala. Unlike our Gregorian calendar of 365 days, this one has a different count of days. It is a living story that moves within other cycles of time. The *Tzolk'in* is widely used by present-day Maya in its pure traditional form, and it is based upon periods of 13 days that interlock with cycles of 20 days, together yielding a longer cycle of 260 days (13 × 20).

My husband and I became Solar Initiates, able to pass this knowledge on to others through the Maya Mysteries School we founded at the invitation of the Yucatec elders. Over the years we were fortunate to be initiated by Maya shamans who followed ancient ways, seeding little gems of wisdom within us that are still germinating. The shamans are adept at channelling or directing solar encodements through crystal skulls during their ceremonies in ancient temples. One shaman and 'day-keeper', Hunbatz Men of the Itzá Maya tradition, taught us to use a beautiful little prayer whilst sounding the Mayan name for the Sun at dawn:

> Father Sun give me strength.
> Father Sun make me wise.
> Father Sun make me into a seed.
> Father Sun make me eternal.

The Mysteries of Time and Crystal Skulls

The year 1995 found us preparing to go to the Yucatán peninsula of Mexico to take part in energy-activations to re-open the cosmic communication in the ancient cities of the area. These places are referred to by the authorities as *zona arqueológica*, and by the Maya wisdom teachers as sacred cities where the ancestors' voices whisper in the trees and their breath lives on, occasionally stirring the dust of ages into mini-whirlwinds.

This conveys a very different sentiment to that of an archaeological zone. It means that an energy impulse still beats at their heart, waiting to be sensed and absorbed. We felt this opportunity should not to be missed since Mikhail had travelled extensively in these lands some 20 years previously and he had been seduced by the beauty and magic of what he beheld.

'Imagine,' he said, 'what these ruined cities once looked like. I've visited a lot of special places that, on first sight, appear to be mostly grey stones standing sentinel over the dust of long-dead rulers.

'When the Conquistadors arrived, chaos and cruelty engulfed Central America. The unique cosmic connections the Maya held were submerged. Nearly all of the ancient crystal skulls in the Americas were lost, but their power was not forgotten. Stories about them passed down through the local Maya as living legends.

'Hence the delight, awe and excitement of archaeological explorers when Anna Mitchell-Hedges found a life-size quartz crystal skull glittering in the rubble of a tomb in the remote ruined city of Lubaantún in Belize. It was her 17th birthday, in 1924. Some time later, as this dig continued, the skull's jawbone was found.'

'Listen to this, from Anna Mitchell-Hedges' father's autobiography,' I said. ' "*The Maya workers performed ceremonies, rituals and dances in front of the skull in the firelight,"* and, *"It was as though a message of joy had been sent out across the Mayan lands." '*

Anna's crystal skull was to become the best-known of all the skulls because she allowed sensitive people to sit with it, or meditate, and for it to be scientifically tested. This is one of the few skulls that is anatomically correct, with the exception of the teeth, which look non-human. From drawings and models made by forensic experts came agreement that it was typical of a female aged 25 to 29, of Meso-American descent.

Many dubious stories grew up around its discovery and what could be seen in the skull. At one time it was referred to as 'The Skull of Doom'. Anna said that, in the past, this precious skull was used in healing or to will death. It was able to transfer power between an old shaman and his younger apprentice as the older shaman was dying. By lying down with this object, the young man would then arise with all the older man's knowledge.

This caused me to recall something that author Drunvalo Melchizedek mentioned in his book *Serpent of Light*. While he held a crystal skull, imagery appeared to him of how they were used by the Maya and other ancient races. Apparently a person was chosen at birth and specially trained to capture the essence of the time in which they lived. Eventually, when their knowledge was complete, they would willingly take a deadly overdose of natural psychedelic drugs, withdrawing their life-force and spirit from their body and transferring it to the crystal skull. It would then become their 'body' for the next few thousand years until such time as another initiate was ready to encode the skull with their spiritual vibrations and perceptions.

After Anna's death her crystal skull passed into the safekeeping of Bill Homann, and today it is called, more appropriately, 'The Skull of Love', but it is still the subject of much intrigue.

Carole Davis is a trance medium who worked extensively with

the Mitchell-Hedges skull. She said, 'I do not know why the Mitchell-Hedges skull became the icon it is today. Is it because it is a beautiful work of art in its own right, or is it the information it transmits? Whatever it is, the Mitchell-Hedges skull has become the benchmark against which all other crystal skulls are measured. Not bad for a skull once called "The Skull of Doom"!'

We Are Remembering

We arrived in Mexico for the 1995 spring equinox celebrations. The day was 6 *Tzik'in* in the *T'zolk'in* calendar. In Yucatec, the language of the Maya of the Yucatán area of Mexico, it is called 6 *Men* (*Men* means 'eagle'). Traditionally it is the day of communication with the Heart of the Sky and the Heart of the Earth, through invocation of the elemental energies of space, air, light, clouds, cold and heat.

We learned that over 60,000 people were expected at the ancient sacred city of Chichén Itzá, where the huge stepped Pyramid of Ku-kuul-kaan, misnamed 'El Castillo' by the Spanish invaders, stands guardian over acres of slowly decaying stone temples, ritual ball-courts, ceremonial platforms and a circular star observatory.

Many people had come in response to a call from the Supreme Maya Council, who revealed a prophecy originating in the year 1475, just before the Conquistadors' arrival. In spring 1995 a 520-year period, beginning in 1475 and referred to as 'darkness', reached completion. So colourful ceremonies were to mark the event, allowing the Mayalands to release a great out-breath of despair, clearing the way for the future. With this action the Maya jumped from the ancient into the modern world of prophecy.

In the ensuing years from 1995 and the emergence of global awareness, we have been living in the 'years of preparation' for the shift of the ages at the point of Year Zero, considered in some interpretations to be 21st December 2012. Maya elders insist this shift is the start of a new cycle in the count of time – not the end of the Maya calendar. In this short period, time seems to have sped up. So much has changed, with old systems breaking down and the Earth waiting to breathe in again.

The Maya elders continued to emphasize, *'We are in crucial transitional times. The fate of the world is precariously balanced. We give you dire warnings of what could happen if the people of the world acquiesce, if we are complacent. All must rise up and become guardians of our planet. As our shamans say, we must become Warriors of the Light.'*

At Chichén Itzá we joined 200 white-clad initiates who gracefully walked in silence, one behind the other, until there was a complete circle around the square base of the Pyramid of Ku-kuul-kaan. Shamans and priestesses added to the drifting sweetness of copal smoke incense, whilst conch shell trumpets announced the group's presence to the unseen worlds.

Most people had gathered because the impassive carved blocks of this pyramid host unique light phenomena, built into it by its founders and visible today at the time of the equinoxes. As late afternoon approached, everyone was looking skyward, willing the little clouds obscuring the Sun to depart, since a completely clear sky was needed for what was to happen next.

At a key equinoctial moment Great Father Sun cast a series of triangular-patterned shadows onto a balustrade running down the pyramid. The crowds sighed at the spectacle. In traditional understandings, this pattern of light and shade became Ku-kuul-kaan, the feathered serpent. It is one of the ways cosmic forces are anchored on Earth.

The shaman Hunbatz Men explained: 'The Mayas understand this auspicious event as an initiation into cosmic consciousness that will reawaken humanity into the Age of Knowledge. By the use of the magnetic grid that covers planet Earth, the solar ceremonies in Chichén will create a unifying intent to activate humanity into galactic citizenship. This will be done by harmonizing the Earth and its peoples, thus initiating a healing process for the entire planet and for humanity, as we enter the age of knowledge and peace. *We will begin to remember the ancient knowledge of the cosmos.*'

During the ceremony that followed, we were embraced by a number of elders from the village of Mayaon near Chichén Itzá, descendants of those who built the original sacred city. Looking deeply into their eyes, we prepared ourselves for a fulfilment of a prophecy that said that, on this day, 'Elders would come dressed in the colours of the Sun.' Suddenly three Tibetan lamas clad in their red and yellow robes arrived, and in some sense they fulfilled this prophecy from so long ago.

Crystal Skull Ceremony in the Temple of the Moon

The following day was 7 *Ajmac* in the *T'zolk'in* calendar (7 *Cib* in Yucatec), traditionally a day of profound, deep thought. The same initiation group gathered at the sacred city of Uxmal for a lengthy, emotional rite honouring Great Father Sun and Sister Moon. It was memorable to us because it was our first ceremony where crystal skulls took an active part.

In these lands the power of Father Sun is actually tangible during such ceremonies. With 'his' rays causing some discomfort to those unused to such heat and power, we were taught to remember how Maya shamans once healed physical and emotional illness by chanting the name of the Sun – *K'in* – just as *Om* is chanted in the East.

By using the word *K'in* as a mantra, it reverberates in one's ears and head. This is how you slowly intone it: *K'in, K'iinn, K'iiinnn, K'iiiinnnn* ... with a sharp 'K' click and a distinct and elongated sound for the 'I' that sounds like 'EEE'. You repeat *K'in* seven times for your body, then seven times for your spirit, then seven times for awakening the cosmic human.

When intoning *K'in* we were taught to feel and concentrate the energy of the Sun in our hearts. Then we were shown how to transfer it by bending down and placing our hands flat upon the ground, blessing the Earth.

Together with other initiates, we sounded *K'in* in the Uxmal 'Quadrangle' which, more correctly, is called Goddess Ixchel's Temple. This was followed by *Ux*, the sacred name of the Moon, pronounced '*oosh*'. In this way the ceremony was dedicated to the unification of the solar masculine and lunar feminine.

We were beginning to remember something long forgotten ...

During this ceremony, the energy was intensified by the sparkling presence of a number of crystal skulls. They were placed upon the stone steps as the focus of our sacred altar. Glowing intermittently from the Sun's rays, their radiance pierced the wafting clouds of fragrant copal incense as we absorbed the Solar and Lunar Teachings. For the first time in 520 years, ancient Uxmal was ceremonially activated from this temple at its heart.

We were remembering ...

The deep symbolism of the moment was enhanced by beings of light who graced us with their company, merging in and out of visible range. They drew my gaze to a long carved stone serpent entwined around the upper walls of the temple, with a human head emerging from its mouth. It is an image oft-repeated in such potent places, embodying hidden Maya teachings about the knowledge held within the skull.

During the unification ceremony I found my spiritual heart actually vibrating in resonance with the proceedings. Spontaneously I made a strong energetic connection between the temples on either side of my head, the carved stones of Ixchel's temple and one of the crystal skulls. It was sitting on the altar, piercing my mind with an intense wake-up call, a high-pitched buzzing 'alarm clock' of a noise that persisted in my head for a number of hours, even after leaving Uxmal.

'Perhaps the shamans activated it to do that,' I thought out loud to Mikhail, later.

He agreed, 'Yes, they want us to remember our cosmic heritage. The intention and focus of the ceremony was for each initiate to be transformed by light. Light and sacred sound, such as the mantras we used, are very much associated with one another.'

My own experience of this crystal skull had been strong. Light flooded into my awareness and I had a 'flashback' to a past time in Uxmal. Undoubtedly the crystal skulls worked some kind of magic upon us all, mesmerized as we were by the beauty of the moment. Finally, not a sound was heard except a soft cooing response from a flock of white doves – symbols of peace.

Uxmal was certainly a well-chosen place for our first crystal skull initiation. The shaman LionFire said that Uxmal is the Earth-anchoring site for the star Vega and the Pleiades star cluster – meaning that it is the entry point on Earth for their potent energies to flow through and into the Maya sacred cities. It is the place where it all begins. Indeed, it had all begun here for us: after the dual initiations at Chichén Itzá and Uxmal, there was no turning back.

With a word of caution, Gerardo Barrios Kaanek, a Maya *Ajqiijék*, a priest of the stars and a medicine man, said, 'We Maya realize that the cycle of light does not start right away. Everything begins gradually. Not like a light where you push the button and the light is on. It is going to take time.'

Our crystal skull experience continued as we left the protective walls of the Goddess Temple. Mikhail and I were walking together with Elmera, guardian of a very special crystal skull called *Ebmnagine*, through a distinctively shaped Maya arch. Then, we gently placed this skull, incense, crystals and ceremonial jewellery upon a colourfully woven cloth, making an impromptu altar.

Eb, the skull, just sat there, serenely shining out intense love-encodements that the ceremony had caused to be held within its crystalline matrix. These encodements could be accessed later by sensitive people unable to attend the ceremony since, in common with other skulls, it could store information. Accessing them requires a degree of stillness within one's own mind. A calm meditative state is the key since, in such a state, it becomes easier to trust one's own intuition, or *in-tuition* – our inner teaching – within our own skulls.

As we prepared to leave Uxmal, we realized that our ceremonies had been closely watched by non-human eyes! A family of large iguanas, guardian creatures of the city, each almost one metre long from nose to tail, had followed our every move as we finally gathered ceremonial items up into our sacred bundles.

As the week of solar initiatory ceremonies ended, Hunbatz Men, of the Itzá Maya tradition, said, 'The waves of awakening and change have begun to roll. Nothing can stop it now. This is a movement to reclaim the great ceremonial centres of the world. To rescue them from museums and tourists, and to return them to the uses for which they were intended. The Maya ceremonial centres are now activated and they will continue to emit solar vibrations to other centres around the world, to activate them so that they might be used in the ways for which they were designed.

It is time, now, to live out our true solar destinies in good relation with the whole circle of life.'

We were present at many ceremonial activations over the years – especially fire ceremonies conducted by Guatemalan Maya people. On one occasion in the year 2000, we were amongst 20 or so directors of Maya Mysteries Schools from around the world, who were initiated into the Mayan Solar Order of Chichén Itzá. The invitation to be present was not from, but rather *through*, Hunbatz Men, for the guiding cosmic Maya wished to communicate encodements activating 'spiritual memory cells', enabling us to interpret the coming Earth changes and to clarify collective positive intentions during the remaining years of the Fourth Age of the Maya.

This is the vital preparation required of us to ensure the coming Fifth Age holds a positive future for all humanity. Part of this preparation is the activation of ancient temples throughout the world. This is being achieved with 'crystal skull cellular memory', primarily by means of holograms 'frozen' within the matrix of the quartz crystal itself, interacting with the higher consciousness of the initiate.

This great occasion at Chichén Itzá transmitted initiation into the Mysteries of the Skull. Our bones are made of the same components as stones and crystals, and we in the visible field are constantly exchanging information with our invisible human fields and with all of Creation. This is how shamans shifted us into spontaneous enlightened states through the space–time continuum, and with a number of crystal skulls blessing us with their company. One skull in particular shone out – *Xamuk'u*, a large Brazilian citrine quartz under the guardianship of Star Johnsen-Moser. It was chosen by the Cosmic Maya and Star Beings to magnify power during these ceremonies, passing on seven degrees of encodements in time-honoured initiations.

This transfer of power was ready to begin, so our *hau'k'in* teacher placed some 20 initiates, all attired in white, in a line. Then, lifting *Xamuk'u*, he held it to each of us in turn, at our third eye, speaking initiatory words as he did so. The power called 'blood lightning' or in Kiché Mayan, *Koyopam*, shot through us.

It was like being hit by the force of cosmic energy residing within lightning. It can be described as the kick one gets through the intervention of a powerful spiritually-trained person, similar to a bolt of lightning or the transmission of Reiki initiations. During this lengthy ceremony, beneath the watchful eye of Father Sun, each person received their secret initiate degree with the *Xamuk'u* crystal skull, a personal 'energy-upgrade' to activate sacred geometries of light.

Past-life Recall and the Origins of the Maya

The power of all these initiatory rites triggered more strands from my past-life stories. Whilst I wish them to remain personal, they linked together the two continents mainly connected with crystal skulls. I sensed that long ago the early cultures of Asia and Central America were related and this had a bearing on the origins of crystal skulls, but I wanted to know exactly how they were connected. As a start I examined other peoples with 'Maya' in their name.

One interesting race was known in ancient India as the *Naga Maya*. 'Naga' means snake, and snake or serpent gods are still revered in Hindu tradition. In Egypt, another, possibly related race, the *Mayax*, mentioned by the Egyptian priest-historian Manetho, were the ancestors of the first pharaohs. These included the 'black' Nubian pharaohs, who continued to preserve their esoteric teachings. Originating in the region of old Mesopotamia, Iraq, Iran and Turkey were the *Cara Maya* who, moving west, became highly civilized as the forebears of the ancient Greeks, while their teachings about the spiritual and physical properties of light were conserved, in part, in Zoroastrianism.

Next I came across connections made by Hunbatz Men, the day-keeper and shaman, in his booklet *K'u is Sacred in Tibet*. He described clear linguistic links between Tibet and the Central American Maya, discovered whilst in conversation with a Tibetan Lama, Karma Dorje. He found the Mayan word *K'u*, meaning the generator or genesis of thought and all that manifests, is also used in Tibet. In Mayan it forms part of the word *Hunab K'u*, indicating the 'One Giver of Movement and Measure' who created the universe at the beginning of time.

In Tibet, persons with an elevated consciousness can take *K'u* as part of their name. The Lama told Hunbatz Men, 'Ordinary human beings or incompletely perfected things do not have *K'u* after their names. Only when the highest stage of Lama teachings are reached, is *K'u* added to their name. Few have attained it: Buddha *K'u*, Jesus *K'u*, Krishna *K'u*, Naga *K'u*.' So clearly there was a connection between *K'u* in both cultures.

From Tibet, whose national symbol is a tree, spread the great branches of profound wisdom, disseminated by the Naga Maya and the Lamas, who seeded teachings in other ancient lands. In 300 BCE, Indian writer Valmiki credited the Naga Maya with bringing Hindus their culture in the year 2700 BCE. Modern Lamas continued holding a particular spiritual vibration through the centuries until the Chinese invaded Tibet in 1952 and, from then on, a small number of Tibetan crystal skulls arrived in the West.

One day Mikhail suggested, 'If we are wise and really want to go on a path of discovery about the greater history of Earth, we should discard our school history books. Then a new reality will dawn and a certain magic of why we are here on this planet will be rekindled.'

I replied, 'I'm starting to think there really were connections between the Americas and Asia in ancient times, and perhaps that means their knowledge and understanding of the crystal skulls has something in common. After all, crystal skulls have been found in China, Mongolia and Tibet as well as Meso-America. Maybe they all originated from the same place?'

'I agree. Our speculations are as relevant as those of other disciplines,' said Mikhail. 'Remember, astrophysicists are telling us about multiple dimensions and not just one universe but "multiverses". Meanwhile, we are trying to connect up all the dots of past and future events, and they are looking up at the night skies through complex modern equipment, endeavouring to make sense of myriad stars and a universe that, against all the rules of physics, appears to still be expanding.'

I looked up from my computer, where I was contacting friends on my new Skullmeet blog, and commented to Mikhail, 'Our crystal skull research is starting to put us in contact with a number of very interesting people, isn't it? We are living in challenging times when we must find the balance in our lives. We need to know when to reveal an insight and when not to.'

I slipped into musing about some of the intriguing answers I had received from a number of the crystal skull guardians I had contacted, who had responded to my questions about the skulls.

One of the guardians I had met was healer Kathleen Murray, who lives in Scotland. Her reply to my questions was quite different to the views of historians, giving me plenty to consider. I had asked Kathleen, 'What is the connection, if any, between ancient Central American and Himalayan crystal skulls?'

In response she specifically mentioned prophecies *from* the skulls, regarding a shift of spiritual energy from Tibet to the Mayalands. This was Kathleen's reply:

> The ancient and the old Central American and Himalayan crystal skulls hold information about a particular Earth matrix, of which there have been many keepers. The keepers have been shamans, lamas, priests and priestesses. They hold many Earth matrices, which are connected in with other crystal skulls, but there is one which they share together. This matrix is very active at the moment and will become progressively more active through the coming transitions of consciousness.
>
> There are prophecies in these skulls about the changing of energy centres from the Himalayas to South America, to ease the shifting of polar energy. Masters and mistresses of many traditions are carefully guarding the light of these skulls until they are all in the right hands.

This information was channelled by Kathleen Murray from Crystal Skull Consciousness and the Council of Lemurian Elders, which come through the crystal skulls of *Mahasamatman* (*Sammie*), *Kalif, Jade* and other skulls in Kathleen's care.

Kathleen's words confirmed something important, but I was prompted to pick up a special natural smoky quartz crystal cluster of mine and turned to Mikhail saying, 'Look, I don't really want to study history, even the history that may have been deliberately hidden from us by academic protocols. I want to study the future, humanity's future! It's a really challenging topic, but I want to probe our possible futures as we journey through time.'

'Well, we have chosen the right people to study with. The Maya are considered the Masters of Time,' Mikhail replied.

'Learning to relax, then allowing relaxation to intensify,

takes us into meditative states and slower resonant brain-wave impulses. It allows us to go deeply into our soul journey and to find that, within our minds, there is a sparkling multi-faceted crystal of perfect clarity and vision. I believe it's for this reason that the crystal skulls are here on Earth. They remind us of something vital that most of us have forgotten.'

I said this while fingering the crystal cluster which had travelled widely with me. It had been activated in the presence of numerous crystal skulls. I felt it had taken on their qualities and hidden wisdom, although it is small. So it is rather comforting when held in the hand. I frequently do this whenever something appears to be out of place or forgotten, since it immediately re-connects me to my spiritual roots.

'There is something we need to remember, something that is as fleeting as the winds that caress the Maya pyramid temples with a perfumed air. Something that is both a remembering and a forgetting, within the dream of Time that shifts us into the future,' I concluded. Deep within my own skull I just *knew* that the crystal skulls held the answer.

I like playing with words, and spontaneously picked up pen and paper, putting together a little verse, a mnemonic. I wrote down in capitals the words C-R-Y-S-T-A-L S-K-U-L-L-S in two vertical columns, then alongside I wrote, Crystals, Remind, You, Share, Talk, Activate, Love, and then, Serenely, Knowing, Un-, Limited, Light, Secrets.

A few years later I discovered that this kind of writing is known to some Native American wisdom teachers as a star-people language because, when you write, it channels a meaning beyond just a simple word.

Let me tell you what Boris Schneickert had to say about crystal skulls from his perspective. He works with IKA-International, an organization in Germany dedicated to exploring crystal skulls.

He had meditated with a group of four skulls named *Rose-Heart*, *Isis*, *Kukulcan* and *Amun Ra*. I had asked him, 'What is the connection between ancient Central American and Himalayan crystal skulls?' He replied:

> Most crystal skulls are now connected in the same light-network. *They are one heart, one consciousness.* Some people feel connected with a special Central American crystal skull, others feel aligned with a Himalayan one and others care for a newly-carved crystal skull with special, new energies and possibilities. However, all of them are connected and, since they are open to share their information, the knowledge is available to everyone who wishes to work for a light-filled and harmonic world.

Then I asked, 'What has been the role of the crystal skulls in the past, and what is their role today?'

> In the past, crystal skulls were placed at secret places inside Mother Earth or in temples or pyramids. One of their functions was to prepare the Earth for a harmonic age. Also they created the structures for today's generation with their energy. Every crystal skull was the spirit and keeper of a certain area of the planet. Some of the ancient crystal skulls help to ensure a balance between energies of peace and consciousness and people. Also they connect the hearts of many, many people, which is important for the new age.

My final question was, 'In what ways are the crystal skulls connected with the evolution of spiritual consciousness?'

> The crystal skulls are working deeply in our inner beings. They support the healing of our bodies. Out of these

transformed bodies and spirits, God-humans are developing. These God-humans prosper and grow and discover
themselves. So consciousness is created. Today the crystal
skulls help us to make an evolutionary jump. The main aim
is to help humanity develop an infinite consciousness.

I thanked Boris for his insights. He had highlighted something
not revealed to me before, that although the skulls each originally
influenced just one part of the planet, they are now connected
with the same light network, sacred geometries and earth matrix
through human intention, and they are 'of one heart and one
consciousness'.

·

CHAPTER THREE

The Teaching Tree

It is spirit that decides whether and when one takes
the shamanic path.

– **PATRICIA MERCIER**, *IN MAYA SHAMANS – TRAVELLERS IN TIME*

How was it that, so long ago, the Maya were able to calculate a super-accurate calendar which needed only one day
of adjustment in each of its immense 180,000-year cycles? Why
did they attach great importance to a 52-year calendar that
marks the passage of the stars of the Pleiades? How did they
know the precise 583.92-day cycle of Venus, or use the advanced
mathematical concept of zero some 2,000 years ago, long before
anyone else?

The true story of the ancient Maya is still largely untold.
According to historians, their culture was built on foundations
laid by the Mexican Olmecs, an enigmatic people whose surviv-
ing monuments consist solely of gigantic stone heads weighing
up to 40 tons and almost three metres tall.

The knowledge of the ancient Maya was based on the teachings of the World Tree. These teachings still exist in remote regions of Guatemala, where I was shown traditional ceremonies using crystal skulls, and I learned how the ancient Maya perceived Time.

Imagine a hidden world of colour and vibrancy beneath the shade of tall forest trees. The forest of green flows like an endless sea, called by the Mayans *Lakam Ha*, beneath a brilliant blue sky. Colourful parakeets skim above the tree canopy, calling out to one another in raucous screams. Small creatures scurry through the undergrowth, keeping well away from herds of wild pigs wallowing in deep muddy pools.

Armies of ants are on the march, cleaning the forest floor of decaying leaves and overlooked by the occasional large and colourful snake, craftily watching from a branch. If you stood on one of the highest points of the land, you would see a few brightly painted pyramids towering over this sea of green, wreathed in mists arising from the moist undergrowth of history.

Within these mists lived the ancient Maya. The classical period of the great Maya dynasties culminated between 250 and 925 CE, though their roots go back at least to 2000 BCE. The descendants of these people are those that we need to consult about the origins of crystal skulls and how they were used, at a time when monarchs were themselves shamans, holding the axis of power through archaic rites.

Whilst much of medieval Europe was struggling with the day-to-day challenges of feudal lords, wars, disease and famines, Maya astronomers were consulting the stars and calculating complex calendars. The ancient Maya remembered their real origins in the vastness of space. They had their hearts and heads in the cosmos, but their feet were firmly planted on the Earth. They respected their ancestors as a channel and connection that could lead them once again back to the stars.

The arrival of the Conquistadors in the 16th century brought a period of darkness when the traditional and esoteric teachings of the Mayans, such as those involving the crystal skulls, retreated. People endeavoured to absorb the new religion of the Conquistadors, paying with their lives for failing to do so, yet also weaving the foreign teachings into their folk myths and religious practices.

Those crystal skulls that were still in use were hidden to preserve them from destruction by the Christians, who regarded them as 'devil's work'. Over the years the whereabouts of the skulls were forgotten. Later, one or two were brought to light by maverick archaeologists digging in Mayan graves, while those found by Mayans themselves have remained closely guarded secrets. Of these, there is a large hollow quartz skull named *Pancho*, and two turquoise skulls emerged over 100 years ago in the Zapotec region of Monte Alban in Mexico. A small green Maya jade skull with remarkable glyphs carved on it was found by a child in a cave in Guatemala, and it is now called *Cana-Ixim*.

Today, those Maya who recognize the sacredness of crystal skulls and the ancestral traditions agree that Star Beings still look down upon them, and the personified gods and goddesses of the Earth add their blessings. They hear Star Beings call out to the Lords of the Night and Day, the inner world and the outer world, to ask them to awaken all humans to the Solar Light.

These deities cherish the bodies of any humans whose hearts beat with the new rhythm of the universe. They nourish such humans with a 'spiritual food' of pure intent, akin to organic food unpolluted by unnatural substances and chemicals. They have one simple request, asking that humans acknowledge the sacred Solar Light emanating through Great Father Sun, who conceives and governs all life on Earth and in the waters that bless its birth.

We were inspired by this great story and so, following our Solar Initiations in Yucatán, Mikhail and I embarked upon a lengthy quest to find out more about the crystal skulls and the future of human life on Earth.

The World Tree – the Roots of the Maya Teachings

Arriving in Guatemala, we went to the ancient Maya ceremonial city of Mixco Viejo on the southern plains where, rumour has it, a very special quartz crystal skull was found in a tomb around the years 1924 or 1925. There aren't any records of it, for at that time excavations were uncontrolled and archaeologists lacked professional standards.

Piecing together the tale, it seems a large crystal skull was found which was kept hidden from the eyes of authorities by the local elders for some time. It would have been brought out on special days and used in ceremonies to honour the ancestors. But maybe because of changes in religious beliefs, or perhaps because of poverty, the skull left the Mayalands at an unknown date, passing from a Maya priest to a Tibetan red-hat Lama, who used it for healing.

Why it went to a Tibetan we can only guess. To me, it is yet another indication that the Central Americans and the Naga Maya had similar roots and a similar interest in crystal skulls. This skull eventually came into the keeping of JoAnn Parkes in USA, becoming known as *Max* – about which, more later.

To add to the mystery about Mixco Viejo, Maya elders have told us of a black stone skull, probably of obsidian, which was also found there some years later. But they don't wish to reveal where it is now. These skull connections made Mixco Viejo an appropriate place to learn more, by focusing a shift of consciousness into one of the threads of Time Past. To explain, Maya day-keepers describe Time as a woven mat, comprised of spiralling luminous fibres. We 'sit' on the mat, with threads from all our past experiences behind us, while coming towards us from the future are all the possible choices we could make. It is up to us to 'read' the threads and choose wisely.

Each day upon this Mat of Time has a different character and focus, depending upon which of the many Maya calendars is in use. In the *T'zolk'in* sacred calendar, still used daily, the day we visited Mixco Viejo was called 5 *Tz'ikin* (5 *Men* in Yucatec). It is a day for ceremony, when sesame seeds are thrown onto ceremonial fires, causing little crackling noises, as apparently a serpent bird flies between humans and 'the Father', carrying messages linking Heaven and Earth.

Placing a small drum upon my knees, I sat next to Mikhail beneath the welcome shade of a flowering jacaranda tree near the entrance to Mixco Viejo. Pausing as always to ask permission of the unseen worlds that the secrets of this ancient city might be revealed, I gazed upwards to this now familiar teaching tree, which I had visited many times. Its heavy purple flowers, dusted with golden pollen, had a hypnotic effect, as I drummed a steady rhythm. My intention was to travel in the shamanic sense – I was keen to take myself into an altered state of consciousness through the repetitive beat.

Suddenly I shifted into a profound understanding of the symbolism of the 'World Tree'. I was shown how all beings live beneath the World Tree. It grows from beneath the Earth, rooted deep in the time-threads of history and prehistory, mythically rising as tall as the tallest mountains and bearing fruits from the buds of souls yet to be born. The jaguar of the night shelters beneath it and the great Earth serpent winds around its sturdy trunk. In its branches sits *Vucub Caquix*, a monstrous mythic bird. This great tree illumines us with its wisdom if we open our hearts to its expansive frequency of compassionate love for all life. This sentiment represents a real living belief in the inherent goodness of nature to provide everything we need.

I stopped drumming, as the sound of bees in the flowers above me increased. Evidently I wasn't going to learn anything about crystal skulls today. But, still sitting beneath the teaching tree, I connected with the golden crystal skull in my head. Going within, I sought deeper access to the World Tree, to find how we might change into enlightened humans. An inner sense, innocence maybe, was coming directly into my brain from the warm pink heart at the centre of the golden skull. The clear message it gave me about Mother Earth was that we are all One, and we need to act with this remembrance.

The essence of the communication simply said: 'The human race now has the opportunity to determine the future quality of existence on Mother Earth.'

The Maya peoples always worked sensitively with natural resources. They used the beauty of nature all around them to evolve their minds, consciousness and love. For us such things may be harder than for them, but the stakes are nevertheless high. Earth's resources are depleted. Humanity seems to be at breaking point. It is only with Love, with a large 'L' for unconditional transcendent love, that we can begin a shift in consciousness, combining the marvels of nature with the technology of science, and leading to the development of a newly-evolved human.

The shift will arise from a personal, yet also a collective vision within our heads, our skulls. When it anchors within us, it will be crystal clear. The shift moves us with compassion for all life and the desire to seek equilibrium with nature.

Coming into balance and resolving conflicting dualities within ourselves is the first step we can take for the planet.

The second step is to realize, as the traditional Maya do, that 'we are children of the Earth'. Let me explain. While *in utero* we absorb life-giving nutrients that come not only from our mother but also from the Earth, Sun and stars. It is both a physical and a cosmic connection that some of us never forget.

Deepening my meditation beneath the teaching tree, I came to understand more. Crystalline energy within my head flowed in torrents of light, and I was shown a mighty flowering ceiba tree (*Ceiba pentandra*), over 50 metres tall, that expanded to shelter the whole globe and joined together the three Maya worlds – the upper and middle worlds and the underworld.

Something was beckoning me closer and closer towards its spreading branches. I could see countless small white skulls amongst its splendid white flowers, shining like lights on a Christmas tree. The skulls were hanging there, magically suspended, waiting for their time to come. *It's the mythic World Tree*, I realized in my deep unconscious. From its sprouting green branches had grown sparkling skulls, holding the souls of unborn babies. 'First Mother, white flower soul-keeper' had indeed been busy in the mythical starry place called 'Precious Shell Matawil', for she had moulded sacred maize dough into the skulls of millions of infants and brought them to Earth.

Suddenly my vision changed. I was in an otherworldly ball-court, and a bizarre game was taking place involving the Lords of Death and the Hero Twins, whom I had read about in the *Popul Vuh*, an old Mayan holy book. Then I saw blood, rivers of it, bright red, gushing from the neck of the twin One-Hunahpu, who had been decapitated. His bleeding head hung in the mighty World Tree.

As I withdrew from this fearful underworld image and opened my eyes, I realized that I had been shown the duality of life and death, peace and war, new souls and a gory decapitated head, and I knew that the mythologies written in the *Popul Vuh* were also written in the stars. I came to understand that, for humans to change, we would need to follow a long, long, road. I was despondent. Perhaps we never would get there, I thought to myself.

Upon returning to the UK, I continued researching. One discovery I made was this: although scientists now generally agree about a Darwinian type of evolution, by looking at fossil records or DNA, they have no way to predict the future physical, let alone spiritual, evolution of humanity. But something urged me to concentrate on the idea that humanity's spiritual evolution goes hand-in-hand with positive socio-economic and environmental changes on a planetary scale. You can't have one without the other. I link this to the call of the Earth herself, through the voices of the crystal skulls and their original caretakers, the ancestral peoples. Today, we live in a decisive time in which those mystic voices should be heard.

By now, I was getting more interesting answers to the questions I had posed to a number of crystal skull guardians. Kathleen Murray, the guardian and healer from Scotland, said specifically, 'There is no separation between crystal skulls and spiritual consciousness. All evolves together, as One.'

It became clear that crystal skulls bridge cosmic and earthly realities, spanning the dimensions and, in so doing, demonstrating their characteristic of being 'out of time' and 'out of this world'. Some of the first important crystal skull research was carried out by F R Nocerino, founder of the Crystal Skull Society International.

More recent research by Jaap van Etten PhD, a metaphysical ecologist, has focused upon subtle energy fields. He found that the number of fields or 'layers' discernable around crystal skulls is 12, while around moldavite, kambaba jasper and nebula stone it is 24, around all types of quartz it is 30, and around citrine, smoky quartz, rose quartz and amethyst it is 36. All of the ancient crystal skulls he has tested have 36 energy fields or layers discernable *and activated*. His research confirmed my inner sense, which tells me that the skulls' energy fields interact with different bands of consciousness and activate specific layers of our human auric field. Whenever we examine them deeply, crystal skulls repeatedly illustrate our belongingness to All That Is, described by science as the Quantum Field.

The next person I consulted with my questions was the shaman LionFire (David R Leonard, in the USA), whom I'd once met at Uxmal. He describes himself as a gateway for many ancient stone and crystal skulls coming out of Mongolia, and his work with these skulls has given him international recognition as one of the world's major crystal skull-keepers. I had asked him, 'What has been the role of crystal skulls in the past?' In response he told me:

Today we use crystals in our computers and sensitive equipment. The crystal skulls were the computers of our ancestors. They were also portals into and through space and time, used as oracles and in ceremony and prayer.

Skulls are associated with death and the passing of the spirit from the living planes into the spiritual levels. The connection between the crystal skulls and the spirit realms is clear and obvious. Throughout the world, beginning in early tribal times, man has used the bones of their ancestors in a variety of funerary rites and sacred rituals to connect with their spiritual allies. Through these ceremonies they received messages and guidance from their ancestors or the spirits and elementals.

The Origins of the Crystal Skulls

Only a few skulls have stories or documentation linking them to archaeological sites. When people encounter a skull for the first time they are likely to ask where the skulls come from.

Although a few skulls have been unearthed from tombs, skull guardians mainly believe that truly ancient crystal skulls manifested on Earth during time periods that are not accepted by historians. Two or three key locations frequently turn up in information gained through meditation, dreams, scrying, channelling or shamanic journeying. The most popular locations are:

Lemuria. Speculation suggests the continent of Lemuria was once located in what is today the Indian Ocean, between the islands of Madagascar and Sri Lanka. Another, even more speculative 'motherland' called **Mu** was also said to exist someplace in the Pacific Ocean.

Atlantis. Many researchers now believe that Atlantis was located in the oceanic gulf between Europe and America. Plato (427–347 BCE) thought Atlantis was submerged west of Gibraltar. Others believe it existed in the region of the Greek Cyclades island of Santorini. Around 3,600 years ago a volcano erupted there with more force than any experienced since. The memory of this massive eruption, which destroyed the Minoan civilization on Crete, may have contributed to remembrances of Atlantis. Even if some of the dates and locations for Atlantis are at odds with one another, the legend has an echo of truth. Maybe its catastrophic inundation etched such a deep memory that it contributes to the concerns surfacing today about our collective future and our wilful degradation of Earth.

Other planets, stars or dimensions. Venus, the stars of Sirius (the brightest star in our sky), Orion (called 'the Turtle' by the Mayans), the Pleiades (an open star cluster in the constellation Taurus) and the worlds of other dimensions are frequently named by people who have worked intuitively with crystal skulls.

In Lak'ech

In the years following my Solar Initiations and encounters with skulls, I asked myself whether it really mattered *where* they came from, since I discovered that the big question really was *why*? 'Why' takes us forward, giving us an understanding of our past and a vision for our future.

Mikhail recently reminded me, 'The basic foundation of spirituality is to be found within our heart. It is not taught, not a religion to follow. It is simply a core *knowingness* which is there from birth onwards. Sometimes dust obscures the meaning of our life-experiences, covering this core foundation and shrouding it in darkness. But remember that the "light" which appears in a crystal, a flower, an animal, a tree, is integral to its core. Its brilliance, once understood, shines out to illuminate the core of our own Oneness.'

I agreed. 'Yes, just like a bird singing the song of its heart, we become ready to connect by singing harmonies from our hearts and skulls. We are *remembering*, changing the song of our light-resonance from present-day *Homo sapiens* to a fundamentally different and enlightened human.'

When you meet a Maya person, they smilingly greet you with '*In Lak'ech*', to which you respond with '*Ala K'in*'. It means 'I am you and you are me'. This is directed to all beings, all things in nature, including rocks and crystals, and it is not just for greeting humans. It would be easy to overlook this point but, time and time again, crystal skull guardians have highlighted an uncannily close and intimate connection they have with their skull – what is within you is within me. They would agree that 'I am you and you are me'.

An example comes from Elmera, an Australian friend, who for nine years was guardian of *Ebmnagine*, a quartz crystal skull. 'Everyone's experience is also that of *Ebmnagine*. No matter who it is, whenever they meet the skull, there is a connection between them, and we come together as one, collectively to evolve. No matter what or whoever you are, *Ebmnagine* will align with your essence.'

Kathleen Murray also affirmed, 'There is no separation between humanity's consciousness and that of the crystal skulls. It is more like two different incarnate forms of the same consciousness. We are all from the stars. We are all great beings who form light into matter.'

I then asked her what had been the role of crystal skulls in the past, and what their role is today. In reply Kathleen brings us remarkable information about Lemuria and Atlantis, again reminding us of our starry origins. This is what she channelled with her group of crystal skulls.

Crystal skulls have been on the Earth since the beginning of time. In the early days of Lemuria there were many stellar consciousnesses that came here to play. They were the original star-seeds from many different galaxies. These consciousnesses travelled in etheric vehicles, which were the etheric crystal skulls. In the latter days of Lemuria the crystal skulls became manifest in crystalline form in the third dimension. Dreamers from Lemuria had crystal skulls, and the dreamers trained for the Dreaming Council all of their lives.

The dreamers had skulls in which they could see the planetary matrices, helping with the formations of fractal light. They literally wove their dreams into manifestation through the skulls. Of course it was not their personal dreams they were manifesting, it was the dreams of the Council of Lemurian Elders. This council represented all of Lemurian consciousness, not only human incarnations, but all ocean life, the animal kingdom and other forms taken by star-seed mixes (mythical creatures). Witnesses in Lemuria had crystal skulls to record all ceremonies of birth, initiation, marriage, death and transactions of every-day commerce.

In Atlantis crystal skulls had many uses, to channel stellar energy in light and through voice. They were used as an oracle, which was not a good idea, for here the stories of abuse of power began and misuse followed. Lemurians, Atlanteans and other civilizations since then have stored information in crystal skulls. This information could be accessed by initiates when putting the crystal skull to their third eye chakra. There were skulls which became the centrepieces for a temple network, paralleled in different dimensions. Crystal skulls became containers for living wisdom, active participating containers which transmuted, transformed and transfigured consciousness information.

The Sacred Bundle and Lady Great-Skull-Zero

Let me take you through a 'doorway', describing how the Maya used crystal skulls in the past. Threads of Time and history mingle, playing strange little tricks upon us, offering tantalizing fragments of clues from which all manner of assumptions can be made by 'experts'. But, like Kathleen, I prefer to follow my heart and, on this occasion, I encouraged my strong attraction for Yaxchilán, a southern Mexican city on the Rio Usumacinta, to guide me. I was not disappointed.

But first, read what Rigoberto Itzep Chanchabac, a modern calendar day-keeper or *Ajkij* of the Maya-Kiché had to say about a 'sacred bundle'.

Wajshakib' B'atz' (Eight Thread) is the most important holiday and festival in the Kiché Mayan ritual calendar. The 260-day *T'zolk'in* ritual calendar begins on this day. It is the main date used to initiate new day-keepers. The new initiate is presented to the public for the first time on this date and given a sacred bundle, a hand-woven cloth bag containing red seeds and crystals called a *Vara Sagrada*. This sacred bundle symbolizes the new day-keeper's sacred mission and vocation, his or her spiritual power, ability and skill as a day-keeper and Kiché Maya spiritual guide. The red seeds in the cloth bag are used for divination readings. The apprentice day-keeper is taught an ancient system of divination based on the ritual calendar.

My story begins whilst travelling the long, hot, straight roads of Mexico, when I told Mikhail of my fascination with a woman who became the last wife of Bird-Jaguar, Yaxchilán's ruler in the 8th century. I had recently gone on a long, difficult journey to this ruined ceremonial city by small riverboat, especially to see the remaining temples. They record some of the finest information in the Maya world, because carved entrance lintels artistically depict the rulers and tell of their ceremonies in now-deciphered glyphic writing.

There was an interesting synchronistic occurrence during this trip: the day I arrived at Yaxchilán was, I discovered later, 6 *Aj*, a day of power, of children, cosmic knowledge and 'the big day of the sacred bundle'. What that entailed I will now recount.

Settling down comfortably in the car, a fragrant perfume of long-forgotten incense drew me into a photograph I had taken of some carvings at Yaxchilán. I let my imagination spiral back along the Threads of Time and, to pass the time, I began telling Mikhail of Bird-Jaguar's wife Lady Great-Skull-Zero.

In our calendar the day was July 1st, 741 CE, but it was written 9.15.10.0.1 in the ancient Maya count of time. Lady Great-Skull-Zero, a powerful person amongst the Yaxchilán ruling elite, with her brother Lord Great-Skull-Zero, prepared for a sacrificial offering of their own blood to the Vision Serpent. Such offerings were commonplace to sanctify marriages, ascension to the royal throne, births of important heirs and dedications of new temples.

The lady rose early, calling women servants to accompany her for a ritual purification bath in a shallow pool beside the rushing river. Then, fully prepared and barefoot, she was led up to an imposing stone temple, called Temple 20 by today's archaeologists. As the sun climbed higher in the sky Lady Great-Skull-Zero was left alone to fast before her evening ritual.

As the appointed time approached she was clothed in a ceremonial dress, heavy jade beads and a headdress of feathers. In her right hand was placed a sharp black obsidian knife and in her left a clay offering bowl. Her servants quickly retreated as the lady's brother Lord Great-Skull-Zero, in full ceremonial regalia, entered carrying a heavy cloth-covered bundle.

Reverently he handed the bundle to his younger sister and she carefully revealed an object that had resided in her family's care for nigh on 400 years. It was so sacred that the lady averted her gaze as she began to unwrap it, incanting a prayer to gods that were ancient even before First Mother Goddess was born in 3121 BCE, during the previous Creation.

As the sky rapidly turned the deep violet of night, the city was transformed, with hundreds of people gathering on flat terraces around the temples. Holding flaming torches and sounding conch-shell trumpets, they beat huge skin-covered drums in a slow rhythm that chilled the lady with fear for what was to come, despite the sultry, oppressive heat of evening.

Thankfully she accepted a sticky herbal drug that would diminish the pain of what she was about to experience. Then she stepped through the doorway, holding aloft a sparkling skull of clear crystal that she had taken from the bundle. Seemingly alive, it picked up the light of the flames within its hidden facets and natural lenses, that caused the eyes, glowing dully, to light up intermittently with an intense radiance.

Lord Great-Skull-Zero stepped forward to assist in her self-sacrifice. The lady poked out her tongue, holding it forward between two fingers, while she stabbed deeply into it with her obsidian-bladed knife. Taking a cotton cord, she pulled it through the wound, dripping blood onto offering papers within the clay bowl in which the crystal skull was now resting. Next, burning the blood-soaked papers, she offered her prayers to the ancestors of her lineage.

For a few seconds the smoke increased, and then an apparition of the ancestor, Lady Ahau of Yaxchilán, the

Lady Yaxhal, appeared before all the spectators. But by now, our lady could see very little indeed in her torment of pain. Trying to keep her focus upon the glowing eyes of the crystal skull, she struggled to remain upright as her own inner vision amplified a million million light years hence, and she was propelled, engulfed in an effluence of stars, to a destination within a distant spiral of the universe.

The light from the eyes of the crystal skull increased. The skull appeared to hover above the offering bowl, such was the ancestral soul-force trapped within it. Our lady, consumed by the Vision Serpent Rite, finally sank to the temple floor with an otherworldly cry.

After recounting this dramatic ritual, I paused to take a drink of water, passing some to Mikhail, as I told him a little more. Some of this had been shared with me on my internet blog and some came from my own inner knowing. I had discovered that shamans kept cloth-wrapped 'sacred bundles' containing many ritual objects for blood-letting as well as for offerings, together with pigments and jade – all items deemed to embody soul-force or *ch'ulel*. They could well have included a crystal skull along with other special crystals. Even today a sacred bundle dedicated to Yaxper the grandmother midwife-goddess is cherished in the confraternity house of San Juan in the town of Santiago Atitlan, Guatemala.

I continued telling Mikhail more about my blood sacrifice story. 'As well as this sacred bundle ritual in 741 CE, two others are recorded at Yaxchilán. I'm convinced that these bundles con- tained a revered crystal skull that was passed down through female lines in the influential families of Yaxchilán.'

I stopped to consult an archaeology book. 'Look at this pic- ture. There's a carving, dating from 723 CE, of Lady Xoc, wife of Shield-Jaguar, whose ritual Vision Rite Serpent arises from the top of a skull – possibly a crystal skull, but this is unclear – held in her right hand, while in her left hand she holds the more usual offering bowl.'

'Yes,' agreed Mikhail. 'Although it was just a story you wove for me, those people existed, and blood-letting events and sacred bundle rituals really happened. Skull imagery is certainly widespread in the Mayalands.'

'Mikhail, what exactly do you believe Lady Skull-Zero experienced during her blood-letting vision rite? I think all those monarch-shamans could slip between dimensions at will. It was probably easier for them in those times, when the atmosphere of our planet was not disrupted by electromagnetic stresses, pollution or the all-pervading fog of disbelief that engulfs so many people today.'

'I suspect that, taking on her shamanic destiny and marrying into the royal family, the Lady had time for personal spiritual disciplines. Her crystal skull would have been carefully guarded in the sacred bundle, and it would have been used to enhance inner perceptions and clairvoyant visions. It would have been used to advance personal consciousness and cosmovision during the rites. Travelling through the dimensions, these shamanic kings and queens actually conjured up their guiding ancestors and made apparitions of a Vision Serpent visible to all.'

Then he continued, 'A Maya elder told me about special quartz stones they keep in their sacred bundles, saying they are "alive" just like the skulls.' Mikhail dreamily recalled how star-travellers, the Ten *Itzaias*, were explorers of our great galaxy and planets.

'Here on Earth they found beautiful stones, advising people to carry them in their bundles, or to wear ornamental stones and jewellery, simply to bring joy. Like us they used crystalline energies in ceremony, and quartz stones enabled shamans to extend their visions and soul-force.'

The Sun was making me hot and uncomfortable in the car, but I continued. 'In many ways, the shaman's ancient ceremonies formed the bedrock of human spiritual progress, and they account for our fascination with the Maya today. They paved the way for an unprecedented evolution of human consciousness, right now, at the end of this Fourth Creation. They showed us how to travel in other-dimensional realities accessed through their clear crystals, and by using their precious crystal skulls with reverence.'

I went on, wiping my hand across my brow, 'A crystal skull wasn't a plaything, and it wasn't something trendy – it was a spiritual tool of the highest order, handed down in family lines of descent. This particular family at Yaxchilán even used glyphs, giving them the descriptive name of Skull-Zero. It indicates they were hereditary holders of a crystal skull.'

My reflections on that family of rulers and their crystal skull bundle were exciting, but it had been a long drive and I released a thankful sigh as we reached the end of our journey.

·

CHAPTER FOUR

Crystal Skulls, Oracles of the Future

[The] crystal stimulates an unknown part of the brain, opening a psychic door to the absolute.

– FRANK DORLAND, A CRYSTAL RESEARCHER WHO WORKED EXTENSIVELY WITH THE MITCHELL-HEDGES SKULL

I had become totally hooked on crystal skulls and wanted to know everything about them. But time and time again I had to learn to 'go with the flow', without pressing too hard to understand them on a mental level. I just had to let my heart and head synchronize whenever I meditated and, as a result, I would be shown many insights.

I couldn't wait to share all this with my friends, whom I believed at the time were all genuinely interested in crystal skulls. I regularly uploaded my blog with detailed information. Internet seemed an innocent enough way to network but, as I dived deeper into cyberspace, questioning this and asking that, alarm bells started ringing in my head: 'Help! Information overload!' It all began to take up a big part of my day.

An old friend, Soozie, introduced me to Karl. I was never quite sure where he was leading me with some of his fantastic ideas, and Karl eventually challenged my resolve to stay focused upon the positive.

Panche Be – Seeking the Root of Truth

As my quest deepened I discovered that crystal skulls, whether of the ancient, old or contemporary kinds, have many interesting attributes. Considered sacred objects, they are used as a focus in traditional shamanic and non-traditional ceremonies, for example by enabling the ancestors to communicate with the living. They are used to transfer initiations from teacher to pupil, and as an information library of a universal or personal nature.

They are considered to be holographic repositories of knowledge, and they can be used for balancing personal energies, influencing Earth energies (such as the weather) and geometric energy grids, and as sensitive metaphysical tools through which to channel healing. Crystal skulls are powerful objects to hold during meditation, they're perfect for 'scrying' (looking within and perceiving other-dimensional realities) and some healers can draw upon their powers as a beacon to guide lost souls 'home'.

Skulls can transfer information from one crystal or crystal skull to another as well as serving as intermediaries to transfer consciousness from one person to another. This was achieved by shamans at the point of death. The crystal skulls are vibrating sacred instruments, giving images or resonances of perfection able to assist in the evolutionary growth of humanity. I will elaborate on these attributes as my story develops.

I had now returned to Britain where I continued to encounter some very interesting crystal skulls. One day in early May Lion-Fire, Mikhail and I had arrived too early for a ceremony at the enormous stone circle at Avebury in England. We decided to go together into the nearby West Kennet Neolithic long barrow, opposite Silbury Hill. This was a particularly appropriate place since, from around 3500 BCE, it was an ancestral burial chamber. We sat with our backs against the ancient stone slabs, looking at some of LionFire's large collection of skulls, which he had brought all the way from Four Corners in Arizona.

He spoke of times spent with the Hopi: 'In some American native traditions the crystal skulls are only for women to use in ceremony, while stone skulls are for men. Now, with the return of the Goddess energy and sexual unity, there is no longer a need for the separation between genders in the use of either stone or rock crystal skulls.'

I asked him about one or two special skulls that I had seen. 'Skulls sometimes have carved images, totems, glyphs, symbols and inlays of metal or other stones, don't they? What could they mean?'

'These symbols are usually clan designations, energy signatures or specific gateways that are accessible with or through the skull. The skulls are also intermediaries between human, plant and animal species. Skulls with carved totems are used to call upon the energies of a particular animal, plant or elemental.'

I continued, 'People who are guardians of crystal skulls say that, when asked a question, the skulls usually give a clear answer. This is presumably to be expected, since they hold information in a coherent way because of their unchanging crystal matrix – unlike our energy, that changes from moment to moment.'

The chill of the burial chamber was beginning to eat into our bones and we huddled closer together. Mikhail reminded us, 'Crystal skulls allow us to access predestined information and even strange physical phenomena such as light energy, sounds or movement.'

At that moment the skulls began 'singing' inside my head, prompting me to ask LionFire, 'What is the role of the crystal skulls today?'

'People I meet are becoming more aware of the energy of all skulls. Their power is manifesting now, to assist the human race through and beyond cosmic time-alignments, moving us into personal, spiritual ascension. The skulls are activators, removing barriers and waking up most people that encounter them.'

'Have you used skulls shamanically, or in healing?'

'Yes, if asked. The skulls can assist shamans and healers to attune our various energy-bodies, auras and chakras, bringing them into alignment. Through further study, experience and focus with appropriate guides, crystal skulls also provide spiritual initiations for seekers ready and prepared for new levels of awareness. Divination and channelling often come through the skull to the seeker, providing connections to the past, present, future, even to the afterlife.'

I was intrigued by this. 'So how could this work? Do you think the skulls are transmitters and receivers of this energy?'

'Sure, these spiritual tools are both energetic transmitters and receivers. At times, the information is so intense that it can take months for the receiver to decipher it. The crystal skulls and the many spiritual tools that often accompany them, intensify and amplify these communications, awakenings and healings.'

We left the chamber and walked back across the dew-soaked fields, ready to go with the skulls to our Medicine Wheel ceremony. I chatted more with Mikhail and LionFire about healing.

'Because of my training as a crystal healer, I've become interested in studies done at Duke University, USA, which demonstrated how praying for people improved their healing process, even when physical distance was involved. A scientific rationale for this distant healing exists because we can access, and in some cases direct, a mysterious energetic force within the Quantum Field.'

'Yes', confirmed Mikhail. 'Prayers, spiritual healing, Reiki and other healing forms bring balance within body, mind and spirit. The "quantum field" explains why crystals, including crystal skulls, can be used as tangible objects for directing healing energies. Accessing some of the potent, mind-blowing discoveries about the "quantum field" makes working with crystal skulls awesomely powerful.'

'Crystal skulls are not for the faint-hearted!'

Crystal Teachings

Being in the presence of our Neolithic spirit-ancestors and the crystal skulls in the burial chamber led me to recall an occasion when I was teaching about crystals and healing energies some years earlier.

At the time I had said: 'The internal lattice structure of a crystal determines how energy moves through it. To an extent this is dependent upon the crystal system it belongs to, also upon its colour. There are now a vast number of crystals to choose from and modern crystal skulls are carved in many different colours. In this workshop you are going to select crystals because of their colour properties to see how they affect you.'

'There are colours for all the chakras, aren't there?' a participant asked me.

'Yes, that is true, but don't be too rigid about it because your *intuition* as to which colour crystal to use is your best guide. As a generalization, though, different colours have different properties.

'Pink crystals give unconditional love. They calm and heal emotions. Red crystals are stimulating, revitalizing and strengthening.

Orange crystals help release what we no longer need. Yellow crystals are active at the mental level. They balance emotions. Green crystals are the most calming and balancing on all levels.

'Blue crystals often help communication, healing and intuition. Dark blue crystals tend to have a sedative effect, helping dream states. Purple and violet crystals have powerful spiritual-awakening abilities.

'Clear crystals such as quartz are purifying, and they focus Spirit. White crystals bring peace. Grey, brown or black crystals are strongly "grounding" and combat negative energies.'

I paused whilst people passed around crystals in these colours and experienced their different energies.

'What will we feel?' I was asked.

'You may feel your body relaxing, your breathing slowing down. Or you may feel your energy increasing and a sensation of a tingle, like an electric shock, on your hand.'

'How about choosing a crystal skull? What crystal should it be?'

'Actually, they choose you! You will just know when you find the right one. Sometimes they only stay with you for a short time before moving on to other guardians or dimensions. Those with highest resonance are likely to be clear quartz, amethyst or rose quartz, followed by jade, which comes in a range of colours as well as the more common pale green.'

These teaching opportunities frequently included visits to Scotland. On one occasion I was invited to go to a friend's house on the banks of the Moray Firth. There I was introduced to an incredible 'skeletal being', carved or perhaps moulded by some archaic process in dark green jade. It was an example of a crystal being 'choosing me' for a short time and then going out of my life completely.

Let me tell you more. *AsKaRa* is a complete and perfect skeleton, not just a skull, and it is currently under the guardianship of

Kathleen Murray and Gillian Ellis in Britain. There is a unique winged glyph etched on its cranium. I was privileged to work briefly in meditation with *AsKaRa*, 'who' is about one-third life-size and intricately formed. How this skeleton could have been made by human hand is unimaginable, such is the detail it displays.

Kathleen was told that it was found in a tomb in Mongolia along with some larger-than-human jade skulls. Explorations in the same region revealed eight skulls along with a 'twin' jade skull (in Kathleen's keeping) as well as another whole skeleton. However, the whereabouts of the second skeleton remains a secret.

All these Mongolian artefacts found their way into China – most likely, according to some accounts, smuggled across the border and, in the case of *AsKaRa*, ending up in the hands of a Vietnamese family.

During my brief encounter with this incredible 'being', I experienced extremely high energy-pulses in the room. Then, closing my eyes and linking with *AsKaRa*, I really felt its ancient origins – timeless and interdimensional. It caused Mikhail, who was with me, to suggest that *AsKaRa* was a prototype of an actual tiny human being whose energy had, somehow, with advanced psycho-spiritual technology unknown to us, been encapsulated in jade.

Kathleen, an accomplished healer, believes that this jade skeleton was once used in collective soul-retrievals (a shamanic term) and the passing over of groups of souls after warfare. But she also believes that 'it is now looking for another purpose'.

A focus of healing and soul-work seems to be the direction many of the crystal skulls are gently easing us into. *Heruku* is an authentic crystal skull decorated with metal embellishments and precious stones. It was gifted to a Buddhist family in the Ali province of Tibet over 100 years ago by Tibetan monks.

Powerful psychic phenomena happen in the presence of this sacred relic.

Another incredible skull I have met is *Zar*. It is hollow and exceedingly old. Perhaps my favourite skull of all time is the friendly-looking *Nefertiti*, carved from chevron amethyst in the distant past, and now kept in the company of *Zar*, *Madre* and *Rainbow*, with DaEl and Laurie Walker.

Back in England, I began contacting more guardians. A crystal skull that had been in storage in Africa for 22 years had recently turned up in the USA, and it attracted my attention. This very beautiful and powerful skull is called *Compassion*, and its present guardian is Joseph Bennett. It is human-size, clear quartz, with rutile inclusions and a large matrix of iron oxide embedded deep within it, giving the appearance of an inner 'brain'.

This skull has the remarkable attribute of a removable jaw carved from the same piece of crystal, which is extremely unusual. It makes *Compassion* comparable with the Mitchell-Hedges skull. A skull with a separate jaw is called a 'singing skull'. 'She' (for the skull is feminine in nature) exhibits great clarity and often reveals pictures of objects or beings within. Seeing pictures inside skulls (scrying) is easiest if you look through their eyes or through other parts of the skull that have sometimes been made into lenses.

Compassion, like *AsKaRa*, the little jade skeleton, is indicating that she may be used to help souls pass over after death. This is what Joseph Bennett said: 'I have been doing work with the dead. *Compassion* is a beacon of light that lost and confused souls are drawn to. This is only one facet of her abilities, I am sure. I didn't choose to do this – I was *called* to do it. The woman I work with said she saw souls rising up to the light when she had a meditation with *Compassion*.'

Hearing this, I had a profound realization about the depths of understanding we can achieve if we overcome our fears of death, and see death as a gateway or portal to other dimensions within the light frequencies. If this was the only crystal skull teaching, it would be momentous, but there was more to come!

I asked Joseph Bennett my three questions.

We are told that the role of the crystal skulls in the past was to be libraries of information about our extraterrestrial homes. I feel that is only part of their capacity. I have found they have the capacity to be beacons for beings in other dimensions.

Another role today is to make us aware of the Sacred Feminine energy. We need to accept that the Sacred Masculine energy has brought us out of balance and into destruction of our beloved Mother Earth, who has given us a home.

If I had to sum up what the crystal skulls' role is for us today, it would be balancing the energies, a spiritual balance between the Yin and the Yang, so that we can make the transition to higher dimensions, as our brothers and sisters are doing on other planets in our own and in other solar systems.

Then I asked, 'In what ways are the crystal skulls connected with the evolution of spiritual consciousness?'

We as humans have the opportunity, when working with crystal skulls, to be involved in our evolutionary growth. Possibly for the first time, we can grow enough to visualize a world characterized by the Sacred Feminine, by Yin energies – sharing, caring, nurturing and giving unconditional love to each other. The Yang energy of the Sacred

Male, which amasses personal wealth at the expense of our Mother Earth, has to come to an end in 2012, and the crystal skulls are forebringers of this message.

Joseph's replies gave me plenty to think about. His crystal skull *Compassion* is very empowering when used sensitively.

The skull was examined by geologists at a museum, who would not speculate. However, a veteran geologist did say *Compassion* was not carved with a machine, as she is not symmetrical. This is very important. Secondly, the area under her maxilla was done by hand. As to the age of carving, no one knows, and the geologist did not want to go on record regarding the date of carving or the process used.

For some years, people have been trying to explain crystal skulls using scientific methods. In 1970 the famous Mitchell-Hedges skull was examined by scientists at the computer company Hewlett Packard, which had one of the most extensive crystal research laboratories in the world. Computer chips or integrated circuits developed there are used in all our latest technology, from highly accurate timekeeping to computers and satellites.

One of the tests on the Mitchell-Hedges skull proved that it was made from an extremely pure form of silicon dioxide, of similar quality to that used in modern technology. It has piezo-electric properties, meaning that, like a battery, it is able to generate electricity. Positive and negative polarities run from the top of the skull to its base.

All quartz also has optical properties, and this crystal skull was cut in such a way that light from below is beamed out from its eye sockets. The scientists confirmed that its separate moveable jaw was carved from the same piece of quartz as the cranium.

These scientists were hard pressed to explain the possibility of a primitive culture having the ability to carve crystal into such precise shapes, especially as it was cut *against* the natural axis of the crystal without the use of sophisticated modern tools. They estimated that carving it by hand would have taken around 300 man-years of effort.

Further investigations were carried out in 1996 on a number of skulls at the British Museum, London. They are reported at length in *The Mystery of the Crystal Skulls*, by Chris Morton and Ceri Louise Thomas. Curiously, after completing many complex and time-consuming tests, the museum staff refused point-blank to hand over the results to Chris and Ceri, and they have never been made public.

Disheartened, I said to Mikhail, 'It seems we can't rely upon scientists to give us full information about the skulls.'

Mikhail suggested, 'Science is only now beginning to understand cosmic influences that cause Earth to be a "garden" for the ongoing development of an integral energy-field. Shamans knew about this synergy millennia ago, in connection with the crystal skulls. So why don't you continue studying ancient documents and carvings from the Mayalands? Deepen your intuition through meditation. It always flows well when you take time for it.'

I did just that. I built up a clearer picture of where my quest was leading me. The crystal skulls were providing me with vast amounts of information, enabling me to cross the barriers of Time. I was also inspired by the words of Carole Davis, a trance medium, who worked for many years with the Mitchell-Hedges skull. She described it as an advanced computer. 'It could incorporate an intelligence but not a personality. Much like the voice-recognition programs we have now.'

By a strange coincidence, that day my friend Soozie, with whom I sometimes travel, turned up on our doorstep. She introduced me to Karl, a tall black American who is a great computer geek. Within minutes of downing cups of strong coffee, our conversation was delving deeper and deeper into speculative developments around the concept of ALTA, a computer prediction model. ALTA stands for 'asymmetric language trend analysis'. Simply explained, by analyzing millions of words used each day on the internet, ALTA is able to forecast future trends based on associations between words and emotional responses to those words.

I agreed with Karl when he said that this analysis is a kind of 'computer prophecy'. Karl rather nervously started telling me about two possible outcomes for the future.

'Humanity, as a collective, has a choice between two timelines. Have powerful governments and ruling elites trapped themselves within a cataclysmic timeline mentality? Or will an awakened and empowered humanity find itself on a positive timeline, achieving self-governance?'

'Why do you say that?' I asked Karl.

'It's similar to Maya cosmovision teachings about the Mat of Time,' he replied.

How did he come to hear about hidden Maya visionary beliefs concerning Time, I wondered? Why had he suddenly appeared on my doorstep?

He continued, 'A study by a little-publicized organization, the Farsight Institute, used highly-trained military operatives who were "remote viewers" to look into the future, in order to study climate and planetary change between the years 2008 and 2013.'

'That's very interesting. I've never seen it reported in the newspapers.'

'Of course you wouldn't,' replied Karl. 'Governments don't readily give away secrets about people who can see into the future, or technologies such as the chronovisor.'

'The what?'

'The chronovisor is very scary technology. It uses a screen or holographic template to locate and display scenes from the past or future in the time-space hologram.' His voice dropped to a whisper. 'According to my sources, it was originally developed by Italian scientists – you know who I mean ...' he said cryptically. 'I am told that, because the chronovisors cannot identify absolute deterministic futures, but rather two or more alternative timelines, they may view either catastrophe or positive human evolution.'

'So it's still up to us what happens?'

'Yes, of course it is, and it has always been the cosmic plan for humans to evolve at this time. Maya teachers speak only of the end of time-cycles – not of an apocalypse. But the danger is that disaster-thinking will embed itself into the mentality of an overriding proportion of people. Then, if the major governments of the world also prepare secretly for both natural and human-triggered disasters, the stage will be set for that kind of action.'

'But look, Karl,' I insisted, 'All the signs are that people will choose a positive path, a positive timeline. We have to ensure that we make the right choices. Ask what timeline we are on. Are we going to be victims of manipulation? Or are we going to work with natural cosmic laws on Earth, and select the affirmative path?'

Karl was holding his head. 'Sometimes,' said Soozie, 'You just can't shake him out of his depressive mode.'

Karl seemed to sense some strange forces at work. Although he would only ever admit to working with computers, I knew from Soozie that he was highly sensitive to electromagnetic energies. He was deeply into conspiracy theories and exopolitics (the politics relating to ETs). It was as if he was a kind of radar, scanning the airwaves, secretly surfing the interface between Time and No-Time. His way of expressing himself was very strange to outsiders and Karl had developed his own brand of the science of Time.

We were sure that he could be trusted. But Mikhail often warned me not to give too much information away on the internet, and he was critical of my constant use of my blog. Unexpectedly, as Karl and Soozie said goodbye, Karl reinforced this, whispering, 'Stop blogging! You never know what some crazy clandestine World Order might be up to.' In my naïveté, I thought he meant it as a joke.

Time and Itzamná – Bringer of the Crystal Skulls

It was time to get back to Mexico and continue my pursuit of crystal skulls in those magical lands of the Maya. I was ready to look into various aspects of the Maya Keys to Destiny, as they termed time-cycles of the Sun, Moon and Pleiades, whilst trying not to be confused by the complex mathematics in their enigmatic calendars.

One day in Mérida, Mikhail explained, 'Of course the ancient Maya system of timekeeping had to be decoded. It was all very complex. The way numbers were depicted by glyphic symbols used in the calendar counts varied from place to place. For example, sometimes a skull represented a number.'

'Yes, I have seen many carved skulls on pyramid platforms, temple plaques and large stone steles.'

'The secrets of *all* the calendars used – some 17 of them – are still unknown since just three counts, the Long Count, *Haab* and *T'zolk'in* are in regular use.'

'Oh, it's all so complicated,' I sighed. 'I'm going to meditate with the crystal skull inside my head and ask it to explain it to me.'

So once again, thanks to my initiations with crystal skulls, I practised shifting consciousness into other-dimensional realities, to access the mysteries of cosmovision. Using similar shamanic skills was probably how the finer details of the calendars came about anyway.

Something 'spoke' through my skull. Dazed, I looked around, then told Mikhail what I'd learnt. 'Hey! I don't need to work out the mathematics of the calendars. What a relief! "They" wanted to tell me about the city of Xunan Tunich in Belize, whose name means "The Great Woman who watches the Cycles of Time".

'I was asked to remember their cosmovision and a profound truth, "as above, so below" or, literally, "as in the sky, so in the Earth".' Spoken in Itzá Maya, this is *Bey ti' ka'an, Bey ti' lu'um*.

'I just love that teaching, don't you?'

Then, consulting the *T'zolk'in* calendar to guide us on the sacred day of 5 *Kame* (5 *Cimi* in Yucatec), popularly referred to as 'death' and depicted as a skull, Mikhail and I drove the short distance from Mérida to Dzibilchaltún, Yucatán. It is one of the earliest sacred ceremonial cities, built around 1000 BCE, and regarded as the 'Mother City of the Yucatec Maya'.

Like me, shaman and crystal skull guardian LionFire had accessed a deeper level of understanding when sensing the energies of Dzibilchaltún, because he relates in his e-book *Secrets of the Maya Chakra Temples*, 'It is the anchoring site for the Pleiades star cluster. During the time of the equinoxes the Temple of the Dolls is known as the Temple of the Seven Rays, and it activates all chakra centres.'

'So this was why my head chakras and golden crystal skull were activated when I was there last year!' I mused.

The shaman told me more: 'This important ancient Maya temple is one of the major crystal skull initiation and channelling sites in the Americas.'

Hunbatz Men confirmed this, telling us that it was where Itzamná, Lord of Day and Night, Lord of Knowledge, Dew of the Sky, Lord of the East, founder of the Maya culture, descended from the sky to transmit wisdom to his people, bearing a crystal skull.

This well-known story was woven with mystery as it was re-told, roughly as follows. 'Once, long ago, it happened in this way ... Held in the sacred memory of the People of the Maize, a great light shone over the land and an omnipotent divine being, Itzamná, looked down gently upon his people, the Children of the Sun, the ancestors of the Itzá Maya. Within the light Itzamná descended from the heavens holding a shining crystal skull giving many rays of enlightenment to all directions of the world. It is told that the heavenly illumination of this holy supernatural event caused Itzamná, God of Night, bringer of maize, to create the Itzá Age of Wisdom.'

Looking up on a bright starry night, lit by a thin crescent of the waxing moon, we can see Itzamná clairvoyantly as the symbolic God of Night, ruling with his consort, the fine-looking, slender Young Moon Goddess Ixchel. You would know if you came across him, because he is a cross-eyed, toothless old man with a lizard's body!

His other consort Chak-Chel, the Waning Moon Goddess, is still respected by Maya women if they are guided to be Skull Priestesses, normally at the age of 52 years. They become illumined with very ancient crystalline knowledge, whilst the great primordial goddesses who protect the crystal skulls bless their path.

On this occasion, upon arrival at Dzibilchaltún, Mikhail and I made our way directly to the Xlacah *cenote*, a sunken waterhole. It was the actual place where Itzamná is reputed to have come to Earth. The clear waters of the *cenote* mirrored the azure blue sky and around the banks was a mass of fragrant water flowers.

We spotted its snake-smooth surface from a distance reflecting a time-honoured ritual taking place. As we quietly approached we could smell the distinctive fragrance of burning copal incense and hear soft chanting from a group of white-clad people. Clearly they weren't ordinary tourists, and we respectfully stood to one side.

Imagine our surprise when we saw shamans conducting a ceremony with a number of crystal skulls! There they were, placed on the flat stones at the edge of the water, surrounded by flowers and with the group already intently focused upon them.

We were welcomed and invited to come closer to participate. At first the skulls were cleansed with copal incense, then all were splashed vigorously with water. Some of the clear crystal skulls seemed to light up, manifesting colours, magically casting rainbows of light down upon the waters, as their guardians held them aloft. Each participant was offered a crystal skull to hold and meditate with. For a short while, a deep peace fell over the group.

Within moments this was disturbed by the sudden cry of a bird, followed by the sound of a shrill whistle as two khaki-clad guards shouted repeatedly, 'No ceremony, no ceremony!' The group gathered around the skulls remained focused. I didn't like the look of this, or of another man who had appeared on the edge of our group, seemingly from nowhere. His energy didn't fit in and a shiver of apprehension ran down my spine.

Standing as still as stone, we all must have wondered about this sudden disruption. Mikhail and I had had other experiences when traditional ceremonies had been forcibly broken up by guards in Mexico, so this was no surprise to us. The authorities seemed to fear the power that indigenous knowledge could manifest, and they were alarmed that foreigners were now attending the ceremonies. Only at remote sites can guards be given a little incentive to turn a blind eye.

A whistle blew again. Its disturbing sound simply drew the

group closer together, protecting the crystal skulls. Looking upwards, we all called loudly upon *Hunab K'u*, supreme Maya deity and creator of all the worlds, the One Giver of Movement and Measure, to bring his blessing and influence upon the disruptive guards. Perhaps he did, because after one of the shamans spoke to them, they just settled down on some high rocks to oversee the rest of the proceedings. The strange intruder who had disturbed me disappeared and I only hoped that he wouldn't cross my path again. Maybe it was just my imagination, but he seemed to have malicious intent.

For some reason, I remembered the warnings Mikhail and Karl had given me about using the internet and my blog site. I continued to feel uneasy about the strange man. To counter-balance these fears, I was learning to tune in to a number of synchronicities occurring in my life. Synchronicities often happen in close relationships, as a kind of extrasensory skill emerges when thoughts or words from each partner occur simultaneously. Other synchronistic happenings are warnings given by creatures in the natural world, such as a bird's alarm call or just our plain old intuition becoming stronger. It made me feel we hadn't happened upon the crystal skull ceremony by chance. There were a number of deep lessons to learn from it.

Sk'ul lem Teachings in Nah Chan

The next sacred Maya city we went to was Palenque, or Nah Chan as it is called by locals. Their elders revere it as an ancient university. Chichén Itzá is dedicated to the science of Time, Dzibilchaltún to Itzamná, and Nah Chan is attuned to the movement and measure of space–time.

This is evidenced by special spherical and cubic jade objects, held in the skeletal hands of Lord Pakal Votan in his sarcophagus – he died there in the year 683 CE. They indicate he had mastered the cosmic implications of movement and measure, in order to transcend Time itself. These objects, when shown as a circle and square, or the squared circle, symbolize the inner and outer balancing of the sacred mind. It is one of the oldest esoteric truths, found worldwide. Portrayed in the tomb of Lord Pakal Votan are beings called the Nine Lords of Time, who are connected with vast periods of Time. They are there to assist him in his journey to the underworld and rebirth.

Arriving in Nah Chan at dawn, we met a group of Solar Initiates as they prepared to introduce their crystal skulls to Great Father Sun, just as the ancient Maya priests, the *hau'k'in*, once did. The day, of course, was well chosen, for it was 10 *Apu* (10 *Ahau*), the day of the spiritual warrior – and it was my Maya 'birthday' too.

We were informed by the modern *hau'k'in* Hunbatz Men, leading the group, that they were fulfilling a prophecy about crystal skulls recorded in a sacred book, the *Chilam Balam of Chumayel*, where these objects are referred to as 'the skulls of the night'. In chapter IV, about the Tests, it states, 'My son, go and bring me the crystal skull of the night'. There is a further prophecy connected with Itzamná, Lord of Night, that says, 'When the crystal skulls return to the sacred Mayan lands, the cycle of Time for the return of Mayan cosmic consciousness will be set up and completed.'

In Nah Chan, time was passing in short bursts, in a very odd sort of way. More than once I noticed time was not always continuous – clearly signalling that something momentous was going to happen. As the Sun rose, the signal came for the ceremony to begin, accompanied by a deafeningly loud dawn chorus of tropical birds.

Tying a red solar band around his head, Hunbatz Men announced, 'The Mayan name of the God *Hunab K'u* derives from the word *sk'ul*, meaning "skull". We ask for permission to enter his divine memory, so that we can understand the reason why the ancient Mayas practised several religions here. During our meditation we will ask him about the best way to take this cosmic Mayan religion to humankind, and also ask him to let the crystal skulls help us complete this mission.'

Our *hau'k'in* taught us that the mantric sound for skulls is 'SSSSSSSSSSS', and that *K'u* is the creator of every existing thing, especially our heads. He said that, when we invoke our Creator *Hunab K'u*, we repeat his sacred name so that it vibrates within our skulls: 'K'UUUUUUUUUU', 'LLLLLLLL' is the sound that occurs when the essence of 'SSSSSSSS' is manifested, or becomes matter – hence *sk'ul*.

The Mayan name for crystal skulls is *sk'ul lem*. *Lem* means light or brightness. It is usually translated as *Le*, which means something that flies or travels. The letter 'M' is known as Mother Earth's sacred sound – rather like 'OM' in other cultures, it is the mantric sound that she uses to harmonize and lull herself – 'MMMMMMM'.

So, putting this all together, *sk'ul lem* means 'the manifest sacred name in our skulls that travels within light and harmonizes Mother Earth'.

The initiatory group chanted these powerful mantras to a number of skulls arrayed on an altar illuminated by the Sun, as 'he' blessed us with a soft pink light. It was a moment of inexplicable magic. There was no doubt that the mantras synchronized us with crystalline frequencies. Sounds washed over and around the skulls as, one by one, they took up the light, shining with increasing intensity as the Sun's orb rose higher into a cloudless sky. It was a stunning sight as each brilliantly lit crystal skull seemed to be remembering something deep within, just as we remembered that we were beings of light, illumined with light.

During the rest of the day, with heightened consciousness, Mikhail and I explored many temples and enjoyed the lush rain-forest of the surrounding national park. We walked across to shady trees along the small River Otolum that runs through the city.

Sitting together on a smooth rock, with the sparkling water flowing by, Mikhail reminded me, 'Crystal skulls have been awaiting the right moment in time to activate remembrance of our true human history and the history of the universe. It is only now that this is possible. Only now, at the end of the Mayan Fourth Creation, can energies flow from the cosmos to re-open these sacred sites and others around the world. It synchronizes with crystal skull awareness, reaching many, many more people.'

'Mikhail,' I said, 'Great Father Sun has caused the crystal skulls' memories to awaken, which in turn has activated our memories. I feel that a great power for good has been set free amongst these time-worn stones, still holding recollections of ceremonies when many jaguars walked the forest paths and shy green-tailed quetzal birds secretly watched.'

'Yes, the crystal skulls have spoken. Crystalline energies released by the *hau'k'in*'s mantras will let each Solar Initiate work with full remembrance of their soul mission, using crystal skulls where needed.'

I must have slipped into another reality for a moment, because I was sure that I heard the soft breath of a jaguar, my shamanic guardian, close behind me.

Much later, we walked back through the gateway of Nah Chan, where dark-skinned local Lacandón Maya in their tradi-tional white tunics stood impassively. They were proud descend-ants of the original temple builders, now reduced to selling obsidian-tipped arrows to tourists. Their women sew intricate and beautiful patterns in coloured threads and beads, almost as though they are constantly re-weaving the 'mat of time'. Sitting there patiently all day and every day, the smoke from their bowls of fragrant copal incense continues to carry messages up to the gods. What these messages are, we could only guess!

.

CHAPTER FIVE

The Sacred Way and Time Future

Amongst the sacred grandmothers and grandfathers of the
Lakota, the shaman of power is Wakan Ha. He holds the sacred
stones, using the energy that comes from the stones most
powerfully. He possesses divine stones, especially Tunkan,
that is the healing stone.

— TRANSLATED FROM *LA WAKA SAGRADA (THE SACRED WAY),*
BY VICTOR A CABELLO OF PUERTO RICO

The message of this chapter concerns the Nine Mayan Lords
of Time. The Nine become thirteen, linking them with
humanity's evolutionary leap of superconscious awareness into
the fourth dimension and beyond, symbolized by the thirteenth
crystal skull.

I was spending many hours reflecting on the meaning of Time
and on the revelations I continued to experience through the
skulls. After all, here we are in the 21st century, an age of technological achievement using the intrinsic qualities of quartz,

silica and silicon crystals to create faster and better communication. But also, we sidestep our ability to resolve ongoing environ mental issues and we continue to focus on financial goals in preference to prioritizing continued worldwide suffering and exploitation.

Some would call me a dreamer but I remain fascinated by the wisdom of Mayan teachings and the light they shed upon the role of crystal skulls in a future, more egalitarian world. At this point in my quest I decided to undergo hypnosis in order to discover more. I thought I would then understand the reasons why I was so passionate about positive evolutionary changes for humanity. So here I shall recount a hypnosis session I undertook, to learn to travel into the dimension of Time Future, where I encountered a state of deep love.

Afterwards, I added my experiences to my networking blog, which had many hundreds of people reading it daily. It had amassed a great deal of information and esoteric teachings about the crystal skulls. 'This makes it even more open to abuse and manipulation,' Mikhail kept saying warily, shaking his head.

Time Future Hypnosis

In 1999 Mikhail and I travelled to Tenerife for a gathering of Maya teachers from the worldwide Maya Mysteries Schools. The goal of the gathering was to recover lost Atlantean insights by pooling the experiences of all participants. Around the globe, we had put into place an etheric golden grid that would help illuminate all lightworkers. Two crystal skulls were present to assist the participants' focus.

Some years later, when in southern Spain, I wanted to consult Alice, a hypnotherapist I knew there, who is skilled in regression.

I had been having a lot of strange dreams about crystal skulls and, perhaps if they were logged in my skull, hypnosis would be a way to access them. Trustingly, I gave Alice permission to assist me into an altered state of consciousness to travel into Time Future.

Beginning the hypnosis, I found I was in the mountains of central Europe, describing myself as a boy with the name 'Little One', who secretly found a crystal skull in a flowering meadow. It was sometime in the future. Words suddenly poured into my head: 'The crystal skull came from the sky, from the stars, but I can't say which star it came from.'

Then Alice said, 'Would you like to ask a particular question about how the skulls help in the future evolution of humanity?'

'Yes. I am holding the skull and looking right *into* it, asking this question. It's a frequency, a form of love. It's keeping the frequency of love, and it's saying that there are more skulls … and they are secret as well. It is asking humanity to meditate within their own skulls and turn them into light, to bring in the frequency of love.'

Alice asked, 'Is there a particular technique used?'

My answer was surprising. 'You only have to take your finger and use it to direct the love. You point your finger and draw the love all around yourself with it, as a ray of light coming out from the fingertip.'

Alice then asked, 'Does the skull on the mountainside help activate all the Skulls of Light?'

'That is complicated. Inside my own skull is a skull of crystal, drawing in the light, and then the light goes out through my finger to wherever love should be directed. It's not so much for people, but for everything – directing that love to *everything*. I can stand here next to the skull in the mountains and turn around in a circle, pointing my finger, and the love spreads everywhere.'

Alice took me deeper into the skull, so that I was completely at one with it. She asked me where it came from. My immediate and definite response was, 'From Sirius. Its guardians are beings of light. They are keepers and watchers for many planets and they are a collective energy. They are not for just one place, or one time, or dimension, but everywhere they want to be, any time, any place, any dimension. They can move and change and they are the ones that we would have called "gods".

'But they are an energy, and they show themselves to me as beings dressed in long blue robes, but they are not physical as such. They are the ones who hold and cherish the skulls that have come to Earth. Somehow they placed them on Earth – I am not getting how that was done. But frequency and energy were involved.'

Alice asked, 'Do you know of the ancient Maya?'

My response was 'Yes,' and I went on to say, 'These beings of light are much, much older than that civilization – their energy and information goes back to the creation of the worlds. They are ancient beings, but they are not fixed in time. They can be anywhere, any place, any time, any dimension. They came from the mind of the One God, to do his work.'

Alice whispered, 'Go back into that time.' I responded, 'I see stars forming. They are popping like lights all around. The stars are moving, twisting, and there is one light which is stronger – that is the mind of the God or Goddess. It is in a great cosmic picture of stars.'

Alice asked, 'Can you pinpoint the planet Earth now from its beginning design, its dream place, or whatever you want to call it?'

'Yes, in the beginning, Earth is very blue. There is a lot of water on Earth. I think it's all water – that's why it's so blue. It has a twin. The tears from the eyes of the God or Goddess … tears, sweet tears are forming our world of water.'

'Okay,' said Alice, 'Look at the Earth and, very quickly, see its evolution process from that distant past, through the present to the future, and tell me now what you see.'

'In the end I see volcanoes. I see red and black. The beautiful blue has gone. The Earth is changing. Why, why is it changing? Yes, it's getting hotter and hotter, but her twin, Venus, is still holding the water. Venus has a different evolution – different happenings there. They were meant to be the same, but they are very different now. Earth is hotter and Venus is cooler, wetter, with clouds, atmosphere. This is way into the future, way, way into the future.'

Alice questioned, 'Are there any beings on Venus?'

'Oh yes, beautiful beings.'

'And on the Earth?'

'No. Too many volcanoes. Too hot, too much blackness and darkness.' I sighed. 'The crystal skulls say they want us to know that, in our times, right now, they love us, we *are* love.'

Alice gently withdrew me from Time Future and brought me back to the present.

Crystal Guardians

My quest was deepening. I repeatedly experienced a spirit crystal skull inside my head when I was in meditation. I had found through hypnosis that I really was very connected with skulls, perhaps through other-dimensional experiences or past lifetimes. I then heard from Lia Scallon, guardian of around 28 crystal skulls. Lia is a singer and sound healer living in Australia, and she is the conduit for the 'Sounds of Sirius' – profound vocal melodies with 'light language' that she has recorded with the skulls. I had asked her, 'Lia, what is the role of crystal skulls today?'

I think their role is similar to what it was for our ancient ancestors. As we begin to reconnect with our ancient past, these beautiful crystal guardians are helping us to reactivate memories that lie deep within ourselves – they are reminding us of our interdimensional and intergalactic origins. They are reconnecting us with the universal source energy and knowledge. They are mirrors to our souls, reflecting back to us who we really are, as they help us to access the divinity within ourselves. They are guardians of light who help us to expand our consciousness, guiding us along the path to mystical transformation. They are agents for healing and teachers of love, who are helping us to co-create a new world.

I believe my personal job with the crystal skulls is to activate them with the channelled song and 'light language' for which I feel privileged to be the conduit. The guidance I've received is that the 'Sounds of Sirius' are harmonizing and aligning all the crystal skulls on the planet into a grid of light. Once that grid is fully aligned, all sorts of people who are 'asleep' will begin waking up to the remembrance of who they really are, and why they are here.

I think that, as we work with the crystal skulls and connect with them, we each become a critical part of that grid of light. The larger and brighter this grid becomes, the easier it will be for others to awaken and become part of it too.

Aha, I thought! *She is one of the lightworkers who has tuned into a grid of light through the crystal skulls and, because of the work of like-minded people, this has been strengthening the frequency of the grids around the Earth. Just as we did in Tenerife ...*

After hearing Lia's inspiring words, I now had some answers. I particularly resonated with the knowledge that crystal skulls are holding a grid of light, a sacred geometric matrix awakening us to their true potential.

It was encouraging to receive such positive feedback from crystal skull guardians but I needed to ground myself again, so I returned to the sacred Maya cities to deepen my connection to Source. Meantime, I continued to write of my exploits on my blog. Maybe, in retrospect, this was my weakness, causing me to suffer fears of being followed by a sinister force.

Maya Masks and the Nine Lords of Time

My journey on the Threads of Time now took me to Tikal in Guatemala. It is a gem of a place, where huge rainforest trees stand guardian, dwarfed by colossal pyramid temples rising above the treetops. In these regions life carries on much as it has for centuries. I was relieved to find that Maya people in Guatemala are now no longer persecuted if they wish to follow traditional teachings.

One day in the rainy season, we stood near the main plaza in front of the Pyramid of the Sun. Our respected Maya teacher, Calling Eagle (whose name I have changed), told us about the many jade funerary face-masks found in his ancestors' tombs here. We were being overlooked, perhaps observed, by a giant ceremonial mask of *Chaac*, the Rain Spirit, whom skilled stone-masons had represented in this important way.

The first drops of rain fell gently, blessing his words as he said, 'Masks say that, even if we are dead, the voice is still alive and we can come and talk to you, and your parents and people can still see us. All the masks and skulls around here in Maya areas exist because of a great symbolism and a great science.'

He pointed at the mask staring enigmatically down at us through the dimensions of Time, layer upon layer of history, its colours fading and stucco decoration washed away.

'Look closely. See, the mask's eyes have glyphs of what they saw and what we will see now. But this is hard to interpret for a foreigner because some things only the elders understand, or only women or only men, such as the symbols, there, on the tongue.' He shook his wise head slowly while we tried to grasp his meaning through all the heavy mind-overlays of our western culture, hanging around us like the quickly forming rainclouds.

As Mikhail and I rushed for the shelter of a huge buttress-root tree with abundant umbrella-like leaves, 'Chaac's tears' swelled to a torrent. Whilst waiting for the rain to stop, it was an apposite moment to go deeply within to resolve or at least partially uncover another mystery that was surfacing for me. It concerned the number thirteen.

I tried to figure out why thirteen skulls needed to manifest, as some said, to save our present world. My thoughts were punctuated by Itzamná, bringer of the skulls, and Ku-kuul-kaan or Quetzalcoatl, who was destined to return to these lands from the east, bringing a new age of enlightenment.

As usual I had my Horus timekeeper-crystal with me, named after the Egyptian God of Time. I placed it down, encircling it with my special shaman's necklace of bright red and black seeds. In this manner it formed an impromptu altar and a focus. It was still raining. A staccato rhythm of raindrops drummed on the huge trees. Small creatures scrabbled in the undergrowth and, way in the distance, howler monkeys greeted the heavy rain with eerie cries. The colourful resident macaws – local Maya call them symbols of Time – made for dense cover, tucked their heads under their wings and wisely slept for the duration of the rain.

The ideas of Harley Swiftdeer Reagan, a Native American medicine man from the Twisted Hairs Society, filled my head. He revealed how in ages past the crystal skulls were kept inside a pyramid in a formation of power known as the Ark. It comprised twelve skulls, one from each of the twelve sacred planets once known to his ancestors. A thirteenth skull, the largest, was placed in the centre to represent the collective consciousness of all the worlds.

I also thought about a question Lia Scallon had posed: 'Perhaps this is the legendary Ark of the Covenant?'

Of course, I realized, feeling as if I had been hit by a lightning bolt. *This was the symbolic covenant made with humans at the beginning of Creation.* I had already encountered the Nine Lords of Time, whom archaeologists studying Aztec calendars call the Nine Lords of the Night Cycle, or the G-Lords, on Pakal's tomb in Nah Chan, noting how, on carved Maya glyphs, the Nine Lords are often represented by skulls.

Now I'd got it! It was all about sacred numbers. The Nine, together with the four familiar dimensions of length, breadth, depth and time, make up that mysterious number thirteen. *So this is how humanity's evolutionary leap of superconsciousness into the fourth dimension and beyond is symbolized – by the thirteenth crystal skull.* That's why the Ark was so precious, and the pursuit of it spans the timelines of history.

As I made myself more comfortable on the damp moss-covered stones beneath the tree, I heard a strange high-pitched buzzing noise. Somebody or something menacing was trying to enter my own skull, taking my mind away from my discovery. It was disorientating and a little scary. Although sitting down, I was feeling dizzy and nauseous as my awareness suddenly shifted into strange dimensions. Very quickly, I travelled to the crystal skull of golden light inside my own head. My inner sense felt safe there. Nothing sinister can access my consciousness when it is protected by the golden light.

Then I became aware that Mikhail wanted to move on. He was saying, 'Hurry up, I'm going to show you the Temple of the Skull before it pours with rain again.'

A Day of Danger

Now I am not one for conspiracy theories, but something threatening was occurring, so I increased my level of 'light radiance' protection. I felt it had something to do with the strange man who turned up at the ceremony in Dzibilchaltún. The spiral Threads of Time were separating into two distinct strands, those of positivity and light and those of darkness and bizarre fears.

They mirrored the idea that humanity as a whole is now at a critical point of decision. We have to decide collectively whether we are going to continue on a time-thread that is unsustainable for the Earth, or whether we are going to travel the time-thread that leads to peace and a positive future. In common with what Karl once expressed, there is a catastrophic timeline as well as a constructive one. Maya researcher and author Carl Calleman makes a clear case for an urgent focus on the positive timeline:

When millions are taking the stand that there is a higher purpose to this planet than just to end in a series of disasters, then I believe Providence will move. When millions are showing each other that they too see a higher purpose to life and intend to manifest it together, then a significant step towards the fulfilment of the cosmic plan will have been taken.

My small part in this cosmic plan was destined to keep Mikhail and myself in Guatemala with our teacher Don Pedro. I was highly attuned to the Maya world of spirit after having had many unusual experiences with him. This time Don Pedro led us into a cave system in some remote rainforest. The large caverns had the typical acrid smell of the bat deity, 'Bringer of Death'. We often found Pedro's teachings were an initiatory challenge! On this occasion sinister forces of the Mayan underworld entered my consciousness, and thoughts about that strange man, whom I had become convinced was following us on our journeys and into the dark caves, flashed into my head.

We ventured further into passages connecting the caverns, treading carefully on loose gravel and rocky outcrops underfoot. I trusted my torchlight but I was now losing sight of the person in front. I was watchful for holes that could cause me to fall, never to return from the dark underworld caverns haunted by Maya gods of death. A chill ran down my spine. I tried to take control of my thoughts, pushing back fearful premonitions.

Suddenly a dark figure brushed past me, causing me to lose my balance. Then a strong beam of light shone directly into my eyes and, *wham*, I hit my unprotected head on an overhanging rock. Clasping it, I reeled back, dazed. I called out feebly, 'Help! There's someone else in here. Who are you? What are you doing?'

But there was no reply.

Quickly, I moistened my red ceremonial headband with water, which turned a deeper red colour, not from its dye but from my blood. I bound my head tightly and, once I found my companions, I proceeded somewhat dizzily with the exploration. Perhaps it was Chaac, the Spirit of Rain and beneficent guardian of these caves, who allowed me to finish this part of the journey and begin the long trudge back through dense jungle to our waiting vehicle.

We were all shocked to discover sump oil was draining out of the engine, black and fast. It looked as if the oil drain plug had been hit with a hammer. As I waited and drifted in and out of consciousness, I shivered as, again, I saw the dark figure looming over me.

Unhesitatingly Don Pedro instructed the driver, in a quiet but unwavering voice, and pointing at me, 'We go back at top speed – we must get her back.' There followed a crazy breakneck journey along 40 miles of unmade jungle track to make it to civilization before the sump oil drained entirely. Luckily every bump and jolt took us further on and we eventually arrived in a village as dusk fell.

What did I learn from this? After all, this was part of a thirteen-day initiatory journey and exploration with Don Pedro, where every day held a profound lesson. On that particular day something important was literally drummed into my skull: I learned to trust that, in the greater plan of life beyond our comprehension, *everything eventually turns out as intended.*

CHAPTER SIX

.

Pyramids and Himalayan Skulls

The gem cannot be polished without friction, nor man
perfected without trials.

– CHINESE PROVERB

I was back home when I began to hear some surprising stories
about Himalayan and Tibetan crystal skulls. With a little
trepidation, I considered making a journey to the mountainous
regions of China, bordering those far-off lands, to discover more.
Since for a long time I had been intending to visit Cambodia and
the temples of Angkor Wat, it was an obvious choice to extend
my journey in the region. After booking the plane tickets I had a
few spare days, and I used them to network with my friends on
my blog, Skullmeet.

I was finding this networking site very addictive. When at
home I felt compelled to keep up a constant feed of news. When
travelling, barely a day went by before I was overcome with the
need to find an internet café to log in.

Mikhail repeatedly warned me about identity theft. 'Please,

don't put too much information about yourself online. There are people who want to send you spam, keep their eyes on you or, worse, steal your identity.'

'There's no problem,' I insisted. 'This is a spiritual site. All my friends are interested in the same things as me.'

'That's naïve – there are malicious hackers that do it for fun. Be careful.'

His warning was to prove well-founded. My friends were interested in the same things as me, but I was to find out that more than one was interested for very wrong reasons.

Pensively, Mikhail went on, 'Some people predate on human nature to get their results. It's exactly what happens with internet chain letters, or sometimes even with meditation networks.'

'Okay, okay,' I insisted. 'I'll be all right.'

I was wrong. I should have heeded warnings that counselled me to remain 'invisible', to avoid giving out my life-story or sensitive Mayan teachings, especially in cyberspace. I was to discover that I had given others dubious powers over me!

Into Asia

To counteract these influences I was becoming more informed about my quest. Every day a little piece of the mystery slipped into place, to be resolved in my own skull, my 'innerscape'. It was brought about by a combination of meditation, dreaming and a sense that something momentous was about to happen. Synchronicities occurred frequently and, finally, I kicked my fears aside, especially with regard to being followed. I exchanged duality for Oneness and unity-consciousness, choosing the positive timeline. I began to open up to shamanic teachings and wider possibilities – or non-ordinary reality as it is called.

Before leaving home for Cambodia I received a message out of the blue from the shaman LionFire. I had asked him my question about the connection, if any, between the ancient Central American and Himalayan crystal skulls. He told me of new archaeological evidence which had now demonstrated that the matriarchal, semi-nomadic tribes who had roamed the area between Tibet and Mongolia were the first societies to carve stones and crystals into skulls, by approximately 10,000 BCE. Many of these peoples migrated to the New World and it can be assumed that they brought much of their culture and art with them, including the making and use of crystal and stone skulls.

Next I discovered that pyramids exist in many places throughout the world, as well as the ones I knew about in Central America and of course in Egypt. They include stepped pyramids and mounds in China, Tenerife, the USA and Bosnia.

With the knowledge that ancient Asian peoples built pyramids and valued the use of precious stones, I couldn't wait to get to Asia. Would I find out more about skulls? I was excited. Where there are pyramids there is a likelihood of crystal skulls, I told myself expectantly. Intuition told me there was still much to be revealed in China and Tibet. Would I be able to access their shamanic worlds as easily as I slipped through the dimensions in Central America? It was all a big question that I had to answer.

Then I heard from a friend on Skullmeet. 'Hi, take a look at this.' A picture of a yellow stone skull with a mouth that appeared to be screaming popped up on-screen.

'Where's it from?' I asked, feeling an instant revulsion at the sight of it. 'And in what kind of stone is it carved?'

'It's a type of jade. Many jade skulls are being found in Liaoning Province, on the coast of northeast China, adjoining Inner Mongolia. It is an area rich in ancient cities, tombs and once-sacred places and, today, jade is still carved in the town of Xiuyan.

These old Chinese skulls are not at all like the crystal skulls we are familiar with, for they are of a different shape with open, almost screaming mouths. There are around 12 or 13 of them, reputedly taken illegally from tombs. They are carved in white, yellow or yellow-green jade.'

I thanked my friend for informing me. Then I discovered that one of the largest known crystal skulls is from Tibet. *Amar*, carved from clear quartz with a slightly smoky tint, weighs in at a stunning 22 pounds. Tantric shamans in Tibet once used this crystal skull during spiritual rituals of healing and divination. Following the occupation of Tibet by the Chinese from 1950 onwards, it was carried by hand on a dangerous journey across the heights of the Himalayas, eventually reaching the safety of Nepal. More recently it was brought to the West.

Over the next few days I wondered what my holiday in Asia would bring, and whether I would manage to persuade Soozie, my old friend and travelling companion, to go to China as well as Cambodia. As it happened, the visit to China turned out to be a dream journey into the remote Himalayan mountains instead.

An Ancient Skull

I flew into our holiday destination in Cambodia, festooned as it was by throngs of sightseers. I was meeting Soozie there, so I dashed into the hotel. There she was, but I nearly didn't recognize her with her sun-tanned, short, elfin-like body looking more glamorous than ever. We hugged each other, laughing uncontrollably, and heads turned disapprovingly in our direction.

Awaking early next morning, we joined a tourist group going to the ruins of Angkor Wat. The heat tired us and the ruins were vast, so we excused ourselves from the group and made our way back to the city of Siem Reap, stopping in a marketplace for refreshments. I like markets, and here it felt safer than many places I had been to. Soozie agreed to indulge me and spend some time wandering through the mass of covered stalls, looking at a vast array of cheap tourist items for sale. However, the market-place wasn't as safe as I thought because, on feeling a slight tugging on my shoulder, I realized someone in the crowd had nearly unzipped my purse. From then on I clutched it tightly.

'Hey Patricia, look at that!' said Soozie, pointing excitedly at a little Buddha carved in shiny black obsidian. 'And look there, there's a skull!' There was indeed an expensive, cloudy quartz crystal, human-sized skull on the market stall, seeming old and somewhat foreboding. But something else caught my eye – something I had never seen before. It was a flat, round disc of stone, with a faded label handwritten in sepia ink, and the word 'Dropa' just visible beneath a covering of dust.

In a deep recess of my mind I seemed to recall a controversy about Dropa stone discs. In the early years of the 20th century some explorers had found stone discs in burial caves deep in the mountains. These discs were connected to stories of crashed UFOs and a race of small humanoid-type survivors. It was even said that a Chinese professor had decoded writing on the discs.

I was definitely interested in buying the disc but didn't want to show my keenness. That would make negotiating a price difficult, I thought. The haggling began. Soozie was nudging my ribs, 'What about the skull? What about the skull? It looks great, doesn't it?' But I wasn't going to be distracted and continued fingering the disc, which had strange grooves across its surface, rather like the old 78rpm records my grandfather used to play.

Passing by the offer of the skull, I finally purchased the disc and we returned to our hotel. I couldn't wait to unwrap this unusual object. It was about nine inches in diameter, scratched and chipped around the edges and appearing to be exceedingly ancient. It was about three-quarters of an inch thick and in its centre was a perfectly round hole. The most striking feature was a continuous fine groove spiralling out from the hole to the rim.

'You were right, it does look like some kind of old gramophone record,' exclaimed Soozie.

Clearly it couldn't be that, yet somewhere in my memory the disc rang a bell, but what it was I just couldn't work out. I ran my finger around the groove, hoping that this would release something etched in a distant remembrance. Nothing worked. Soozie and I even lit some candles and incense and went into a meditation, holding the disc between us in upturned hands. Finally we decided to go back to the market the next day and talk to the stallholder. Maybe he had some information, and perhaps between us we might be able to afford to buy the old crystal skull as well.

That night I slept intermittently. I think I was too excited by the day's events. I dreamt repeatedly of tiny people whispering the word 'Dropa' to me, slowly.

The next day the stallholder, once assured of our sincerity, and helped by the gift of a few dollars, talked quietly to an interpreter we had taken along. The stallholder's name was Wei Long, meaning 'dragon' in Chinese. He said he had bought the disc, the skull and other artefacts from an old man from Sichuan province, who had travelled to Tibet when he was young. Wei Long began to weave a wonderful story about him. But was it just travellers' tales, or fact? It went something like this, and was so ingrained in the mind of the stallholder that he told it in the first person.

'I climb and climb. I walk so very far from my original path that, when I look back, all I see were mountains closing in upon me, just like the snow that was covering my footprints. I was cold, so cold. I had to find somewhere to rest. I climb higher and higher, snow falling thickly. Then I see a cave. I crawl inside, away from bitter cold wind, and looked around 'cos I was in a strange, square chamber cut out of rock.

'Next day I walk further inside. Then I find treasure cave. Even rocks were made of sparkling stones. In dim light, I see broken pottery and smoke-stained walls. I kneel down and I use my hands and look for golden treasure. But, believe me, lady, there is no gold. Just discs, many, many, all piled up, all different size. I look carefully. I see a spiral groove cut into each, and each has a continuous line of tiny symbols. When I go to pick up the discs, wow, loud buzzing, like bees from a hive. Bzzzzz! It was coming all around me. Lady, I tell you, it was scary, cos I had woken up the ancestors. I got out quick, very, very quick.'

'Why did he go climbing in those mountains?'

'Cos he was a treasure seeker. It was said, many secrets of lost civilizations and hoards of treasure to be found in the mountains, for those who dare. In those days, people lived however they could. Silk Route through Orient still in use, and many well-worn paths led to it – paths that lead from the high mountains of Tibet, themselves right through to China. Paths that cause a man to risk his life for uncertain gains. Paths that lead to death.'

'So the treasure hunter became rich?' I asked.

'No, he so scared by buzzing noise that he bring back only a few discs and this crystal skull. I pay him just a little, cos they seem worthless. No interest in them. That is, till you came along.'

I suddenly had an uneasy feeling. I didn't want a repeat of yesterday's scare, and looked around. On the far side of the market I saw a tall man, maybe American, judging by his short haircut, dressed in a light tropical suit and black wraparound shades. Beside him was a local barefooted man, who seemed to be arguing and gesticulating in our direction. Soozie nudged me. 'That's the man who tried to rob you yesterday. Time we were not here.'

'Not before we buy this old crystal skull,' I insisted.

That evening, I carefully held the stone disc, running my finger around the groove. I was deep in thought. Then I set the disc in front of the heavy old crystal skull that we had finally bought at an exorbitant price. Suddenly it hit me, a kind of buzzing noise, but whether it was in the room or in my head I couldn't tell. I realized the buzzing was connected with the disc. My hearing is pretty good and the sound was very high-pitched.

It was communicating in a very odd way. I was convinced it was an archaic form of energy 'speaking' right inside my own skull. It didn't give me words, but pictures and colours that jumped in and out of my consciousness in an erratic, staccato manner. If I could describe a hologram inside my head, then this would be it! It wasn't a pleasant experience, nor one I would be eager to repeat, but somehow the energy had a message to give to the world about the coming years and how all things were connected. It seemed to be confirming that I needed to travel to a distant region of China with Soozie to see the pyramids there. She, like me, is an adventurer at heart.

China? Not a bad idea, I thought, especially since I was keen to make contact with shamans who still live in the remote mountains between China and Tibet. I now desperately wanted to know if they had ever seen any discs or crystal skulls. But first, we made up two separate parcels, one for the disc and one for the skull, and posted them back home. We didn't want to risk being accused of stealing objects from China. Who knows what complications that might have caused!

Dreamtime

Two days later we boarded a plane bound for Beijing, then on to Xi'an, a central region where some of the world's largest pyramids are to be seen on the Qin Chuan Plains, amongst fields of crops.

Xi'an, the ancient Sian-Fu, was once the capital of imperial China. In 1974 it became a tourist destination when the famous army of terracotta warriors was found nearby. However, few, if any, visitors are shown the large pyramid just a mile or so away, or told of the existence of over 38 of them in the area. If anyone asks, they are inscrutably informed they were burial mounds containing tombs or mausoleums to the emperors. No one in authority would admit that they could be much, much older.

Soozie and I wanted to see these enormous flat-topped pyramids for ourselves. One was reputedly as large as the Pyramid of the Sun at Teotihuacán in Mexico. We weren't too keen on an interpreter trailing around with us, when all we wished for was to sit on the summit and 'feel the vibes'. We needed to work out a plan. We would give our interpreter the slip the next morning, hire a taxi and head off to the pyramids on our own.

Next morning came. All went well and, feeling like errant schoolgirls, we sped away, past a small pyramid near the airport and on to the tomb of Empress Wu of the T'ang dynasty. It's inside the largest pyramid in the region. Soozie reminded me of records that speak of emperors descending from heaven on flying dragons. We spent a number of hours at the pyramid, meditating with crystals we took with us and concentrating our thoughts on the flying dragons. Then it was time to go.

That night, as Soozie and I slept, my dreams were vivid and quite disturbing. These are my notes about one of these dreams.

We arrived at a small town, which I sensed was in Tibet. Wei Long, the Chinese stallholder, was in my dream. He smilingly produced supplies and warm clothes, whilst hidden in my luggage were the stone disc and the heavy crystal skull. In the dream it seemed the most natural thing to do, to travel with him and Soozie in a very strange country.

I could tell that it was springtime. Snowmelt was overfilling the rivers and cascading down the mountains. Every time we tried to move out of the town we were stopped by floods and landslides. Finally we settled down to wait for the weather to improve. Wei Long, our 'dragon man', was still smiling despite the cold and the worsening weather conditions. All of this took place very quickly in dreamtime.

Soozie and I were holding the stone disc between our upturned hands, but it was only when I put it in front of the newly-found crystal skull that the strange vibrating sound filled my head again, and images spontaneously began ranging across my inner vision. It seemed to be emphasizing, 'Nine, remember nine.' What this meant I didn't know, because in dreams you can't rationalize your thoughts.

In the dream a long period of time seemed to pass, but in reality it was probably only a moment or two. Everything was becoming darker. We followed Wei Long through shabby backstreets. But something not quite wholesome, something evil, was stalking us in the shadows. As we started walking through terraced growing areas out towards the foothills, I saw a faint light up ahead, seemingly beckoning us towards its glow.

We arrived at what was little more than a goat-herder's shack. We were confronted by an old man. *He's a shaman*, I thought. He was in a traditional robe, with a colourful woolly hat pulled low over his head, and he was wearing a kind of necklace of polished brass discs, a *toli*, which acts like armour, deflecting spirit attack, reflecting light to blind spirits and also absorbing energy from the universe to increase shamanic power. Its brilliance was causing me to feel very disorientated. I sensed it was catching the evil that was stalking us.

Then I saw the shaman's face right there in front of me – more Tibetan than Chinese-looking. In response to Wei Long's almost lyrical speech, he just grunted.

Wei was pulling on my arm, placing the disc and crystal skull upon a low altar bedecked with candles and smouldering incense cones. Immediately something happened. I was assailed by the loudest hum I had ever heard, emanating from the disc. The shaman's face started contorting while he twirled his body around, shaking the brass *toli* necklace violently and wielding a symbolic double-ended metal *dorje* or thunderbolt. He was talking loudly now – not in Chinese, but maybe it was Tibetan or a spirit language – calling some kind of energy into the room.

I could feel the presence of a thousand eyes watching what was taking place. Suddenly he was rushing towards the altar, picking up a vicious-looking knife. It had a three-sided blade. I realized it was a *phurba* or Himalayan thundernail, used in rituals to subdue the most malevolent of entities.

Then, being a dream, everything started to get muddled up. I saw snow and more snow. I saw the watching eyes again. I saw that Soozie was alarmed by the presence of the knife – I could feel her fear. She was shrinking back into the shadows of the room alongside Wei Long, who took a protective stance in front of her.

Meanwhile the shaman continued to twirl and shake. A whirlwind of colours funnelled through my sleeping consciousness – red, blue, black, red, with sparks of white light. For one fearful moment I thought the shaman was lunging at Soozie with the knife, but he turned instead and embedded it in the central hole of the stone disc upon the altar.

Instantaneously, in my inner vision, a dark green malicious light shot from the disc, spiralled upwards and was sucked towards the open door of the stove. The fire blazed and crackled, lighting the room with sudden intensity. Soozie was screaming. I wanted the dream to end but couldn't wake. I was screaming too. I still couldn't wake.

The humming noise from the disc changed into a harmonious chant, sounding somewhat like the Tibetan mantra of compassion, *Om mani padme hum*. Then the words 'Nine, remember the number nine.' The shaman's energy increased. I could see his inner light getting stronger, his gibberish words and chanting becoming louder, and it seemed he was entering a deep trance state, but all the while continuing to twirl and shake ...

I was waking up, pulling myself out of the dream. I remembered 'Nine, the number nine'. Finally I opened my eyes. Moonlight was flooding into our room.

Next morning Soozie and I agreed that my dream was prophetic in nature, encapsulating many of our fears about going to Tibet. All that we really wanted to do was to return home to normality and take care of the skull and disc.

In the following weeks I tried to find out more about the number nine. It seemed important to pursue all of the clues, and my queries were partially answered when an oriental friend brought a Buddhist monk to our house, introducing him as his cousin. After tea and pleasantries, it was the moment to ask about the Nine Worlds of Buddhism.

The monk elaborated, 'The ninth is the highest level humanity can go at present. It is the level of great spiritual teachers, lower angelic beings and guiding spirits.'

'It is explained in the Lotus Sutra isn't it?' questioned Mikhail.

'Yes, that's right, the principle of Buddhahood as a potential within the nine worlds means that the beings of the nine worlds, those we might call deluded, inherently possess the state of Buddhahood and can manifest Buddhahood within their lives.'

These wise words again tied together some of the similarities between spiritual teachings in the East and West that Hunbatz Men had first drawn our attention to.

After the monk had left, Mikhail said excitedly to me, 'In unknown epochs and through into historical times a spiritual impulse, an illumination, has reached Earth. Think of it as a ray of sacred knowing that beams into those ready to receive it and anchors into the land itself. Sometimes the main focus of this illumination has shifted location, leaving behind a great mysterious reservoir of enlightened teachings. This happened with those distant civilizations of Lemuria and Atlantis, as well as the wisdom-keepers of ancient Egypt and Greece, the rich Hindu traditions, the teachings of Buddha and the Christ, amongst many others.'

'So,' I said, sensing the importance of what Mikhail was saying, 'At some point when a strong transformative spiritual impulse encompassed both Tibet and the Americas, great wisdom began pouring out from the teachers in those lands.'

'Yes. Today we see their spiritual influence and a radical change in consciousness coming about, because of a few influencing the many. Over the ages probably just a handful of people with higher intent and lifelong dedication have carried out their soul mission to bring in and anchor this higher consciousness, leading to revelations concerning the ninth dimensional level that crosses barriers of race, time and space.'

'I understand,' I said. 'That's why old crystal skulls have been revealed in China and Tibet. Most of them have now been distributed around the world and are in the hands of capable healers with a mission to support Earth and humanity. Skulls from different origins are now coming together. The ancient Himalayan ones, with ancient Mayan or Atlantean ones, and newly-carved skulls that are ready to be programmed with new consciousness.

'If we look through evolutionary eyes, we will see the unfold-ment of a 600-million-year progression of life on Earth, from the first multi-cellular fauna to modern humans. It is a journey of transformation where, according to biologists, the history of life tends to move in quick and quirky episodes rather than by gradual evolution. It is pushing us forward to birth within our-selves and within our times a universal human, capable of co-evolving with nature and co-creating with Great Spirit.'

This new humanity I began to call *Homo spiritus*. Hardly a day was to go by from then on without my thinking about what, or who, could actually evolve.

.

CHAPTER SEVEN

Timelines

The coming of a spiritual age must be preceded by the
appearance of an increasing number of individuals who are no
longer satisfied with the normal intellectual, vital and physical
existence of man, but perceive that a greater evolution is the real
goal of humanity and attempt to effect it in themselves, to lead
others to it, and to make it the recognized goal of the human
race. In proportion, as they succeed, and to the degree to which
they carry this evolution, the yet unrealized potentiality which
they represent will become an actual possibility of the future.

– **SRI AUROBINDO**, MYSTIC AND TEACHER

Following our exploits in China, I left Soozie to return to Spain
and I met up with Mikhail in the UK to await delivery of the
skull and the Dropa disc. The disc never actually arrived in the
post and could not be traced. Soozie agreed that I could keep
the skull for a while and be its guardian. I used this opportunity
to continue research into our human skulls, as well as enjoying
time in a crop circle in England.

The circles are complex patterns up to 500m (1,625ft) in length that have been mysteriously appearing around the world, usually arriving overnight in fields of growing wheat or other grain plants. These enigmatic patterns started appearing in large numbers in the late 1980s and the southern part of England particularly attracts numerous crop circles every summer, each of increasing design complexity. Occasionally, rapidly moving balls of light have been seen after the crops have been delicately bent down and research indicates some type of pulsed microwave is involved in the formation of crop circles, which seems to be almost instantaneous. For example, the complex fractal 'Julia Set' formation that appeared close to Stonehenge in 1996, 151m (500ft) in diameter and comprising 149 individual circles, formed in a time-window of just 15 minutes' duration.

The Sacred Pyramid in the Head

Mikhail and I were sitting early one morning on a small hillock overlooking an amazing circular pattern of flattened wheat forming a crop circle. Just across the main road stood the impos- ing megalithic stones of Stonehenge, strange sentinels for the even stranger crop circles. Some people drove up in a car and took out baggages of photographic equipment. The crop pattern was newly made, having inexplicably appeared the previous afternoon, and they wanted to get some good photographs and measurements before the field became too busy with a rush of 'croppies'.

Years before I had been given a 'download' of light information when sitting in a crop circle. Very often the formations appear in fields sited over deep natural underground water aquifers. The astonishing information I received was that the crop patterns are multi-dimensional imprints, rather like our DNA, which are being implanted into crops, water and soil in order to preserve the body of Earth herself should humans continue on their destructive path. This reserve of 'Earth DNA' acts in a similar way to a dose of homeopathic medicine carrying special vibrational frequencies.

Exactly how the frequency was encoded, or who the circle-makers are, was not revealed to me at that time. However, with my new companion, the Himalayan crystal skull, now by my side I was quietly expectant. Just like the skulls, crop circles are a mystery not easily explained by rational means but in some way they interact if we are able intuitively to refine our consciousness.

The realizations that happened over the next few hours were either prompted by the 'circle-makers' or by the skull, I'm not sure which. Placing the skull beside us on the grass that swept like an emerald carpet toward the Neolithic remains, I thought about some of the scientific research I had been looking into.

Bringing a quartz crystal of any size or shape close to the body always immediately causes a response, activating the nearest subtle energy points or chakras. Crystalline energy can change the secretions of related endocrine glands, as well as altering blood pressure and mental, physical and emotional responses. So the resonant properties of crystals can bring the human body into equilibrium.

Biological research now proves that not every informational 'message' received through crystals is directed to our brain. Instead, minute microtubules in our cells communicate instantly by the tiniest pulses of light, in addition to and separate from bio-electrical nerve circuits and chemical impulses. To a certain extent each part of our body is conscious. Quantum science even says that we have an ability to connect with and are part of a 'global brain' extending into the electromagnetic field of our planet. I have been prompted to think of it as a vast crystalline skull brain.

My thoughts were interrupted momentarily as crystal skulls came into focus. They are guiding us as potently charged and active tools with catalytic properties, reflecting deepening levels of consciousness. Crystal skulls and our own skulls talk to each other! These beautiful and symbolic objects do this and much more, for they are keys that unlock memories of ancient initiatory processes, using three specific points which make a pyramid shape of light inside the head – the Third Eye, the Crown and the Alta Major chakra at the base of the skull. When these three points are intentionally activated and balanced together, they shift us into superconscious *theta* healing states through the Crown chakra.

According to ancient yogic teaching, within the centre of this sacred pyramid, precisely at the midpoint of the brain (if one draws an imaginary line between the Third Eye and the Alta Major chakra), lies the *sunya desha*, described as the 'source of the radiant ether where all that is not pure gold is instantly destroyed'. Let me explain further from a scientific perspective. Both the pituitary and pineal glands within this pyramid respond to light and are implicit in sleep patterns and the release of hormones. Incredibly, because they produce their own hallucinogenic chemicals, they are linked to our increasing extrasensory abilities as well.

So it is profoundly important to recognize that yogic teachings and medical science indicate that the biblical 'place of the skull', will ultimately reveal its significance to human evolution. We simply need to unlock its potential. It's all a great mystery – just like the crystal skulls and the crop circles.

Mikhail nudged me in the ribs, 'Are you awake?' He made me jump, but I retorted, 'Of course I am!'

Mikhail had been quietly meditating on the intricate crop circle pattern spread out on the field below us. Now his energy had changed and, in his practical way, he wanted to remind me of a simple method to balance the sacred pyramid within our skulls.

'As you go to sleep, gently focus upon the *Ajna* chakra, the Third Eye at the centre of your brow, because it will bring a feeling of wellbeing. You see, when you are sleeping, the Alta Major chakra also becomes active, especially during deep dream states, when it releases old patterns and *karma* – an essential prerequisite for a new humanity.'

'Thanks, I will remember that, so that I can do this spiritual work even as I sleep.'

'Remember also,' he said, 'These head chakras are receiving a rich "food", consisting of increasing levels of ultraviolet light and cosmic rays that are reaching Earth because of damage to the ionosphere that formerly shielded us.'

Turning to him, I asked meaningfully, 'Do you think that this increased ultraviolet light will trigger the evolution of consciousness, or even generate a different physical kind of human being?' In reply he simply nodded knowingly.

All this is not so far-fetched as you might think, when you consider the implications of a rare form of ultraviolet light that arises from the M42 Nebula in the constellation of Orion. In 1997 an international team of astronomers stated that sources of ultraviolet light are very unusual in the cosmos. They discovered that the light emanating from M42 is circularly polarized and, as such, it determines chemical reactions instrumental in creating a predominant directional spin of DNA on Earth. According to scientists, this polarization, which appears to be right-handed, *accounts for the left-handed spin of amino acids, the building blocks of all life on Earth.* It is mind-bending stuff! Centuries ago the ancient Maya knew of M42 as the 'Pyramidal Temple House of

Hunab K'u', whom they also know as 'the One Giver of Movement and Measure'.

> *Hunab K'u* said: 'Take care of the light that I leave within my temple. Within, humans will find the light they need for eternal life.'
>
> Only through solar initiation can the sleeping body of mankind be awakened. The reincarnated teachers of the new Age of Aquarius implore the sacred human race to wake up, so that they can fulfil their sacred destiny of being the true sons and daughters of the cosmic light.
>
> The time of knowledge is approaching; the light in the centre of the pyramidal house of *Hunab K'u* will flash like lightning, that will pierce through the shadows that cover the human race. Let us prepare to receive the light of knowledge that comes from *Hunab K'u*, transcend into the memory of the Creator and become beings of eternal luminosity.

This comes from *The Sacred Manuscript of K'altun*, reproduced by permission of Hunbatz Men of the Itzá Maya tradition. It appears in full in my book *Maya Shamans – Travellers in Time*. *Beings of eternal luminosity*, I thought, *how beautiful that would be*. But I am of a practical nature as well as Mikhail, and I knew that the coming years wouldn't be an easy ride for humanity.

A bird's sweet song, probably from one of the many skylarks rising on thermals of air, interrupted our conversation. Gazing across the field of shimmering wheat, with its complex circular crop pattern, I smiled at Mikhail then gently stroked the Himalayan skull. The crystalline matrix within it was reflecting the sky, and little rainbows shimmered inside. The skull was communicating. I intuited 'she' needed a name and, at that moment, my thoughts jumped back to the Himalayas and the possibility that the Dropa people associated with the strange stone discs were the founders of the fabulous lost city of Shangri-La.

'The skull's name is *Shangri-La*,' I told Mikhail excitedly.

The name was perfect, and I was so excited by all that *Shangri-La* had helped us access here, overlooking the crop circle, that I immediately wanted to go back to my computer to give out the information on my blog. Later, when I logged in, I picked up amazing news about a crystal skull that becomes particularly activated when a photograph of the M42 Nebula is placed upon it. Others had posted photographs of old skulls with elongated craniums, calling them extraterrestrial. Someone else was enthusing about a crystal skull allegedly under the left foot of the Sphinx in Egypt. This I thought highly unlikely.

Mikhail was even more sceptical, imploring me not to keep on with the blog. 'Look, sitting in raptures looking at the crop circles labels us as crazy in some people's eyes. You just don't know what you're getting into with that blog. I've still got an uneasy feeling about it. What we are touching into is something very precious, very important to the spiritual survival of humanity. Who knows what forces might try to stop us? Nobody can expect an easy path toward evolving into *Homo spiritus*!'

Day of the Dead, and Stone Skulls

Eventually Mikhail and I needed to get back to Mexico, for I knew there were more hidden keys to the mysteries of the skulls and of Time to access there. A quirk of fate meant we arrived in Mérida, Yucatán's capital, for the Day of the Dead celebrations on November 1st, involving numerous skulls! The day was 13 *Aj* in the *T'zolk'in* calendar (13 *Ben* in Yucatec).

Thirteen is one of the Maya power numbers and *Aj* means 'victory of life over death and all kinds of evilness'. It is a symbol of resurrection, a day of renewal, purification and rebirth. Throughout Mexico, on the Day of the Dead, skulls made out of chocolate or sugar are given as offerings for deceased relatives, inscribed with the recipient's name on the forehead. It is traditional for relatives to sit all night beside graves or beside altars bedecked with flowers and candles, specially made for the occasion.

I was drawn to buy a bunch of orange marigolds to make a personal Day of the Dead *ofrenda* around the crystal skull *Shangri-La* in our hotel room. Our spirits were lifted every morning as we went to get our breakfast tortillas (flat maize pancakes), smiling as we passed a tourist shop that said 'Broken English spoken perfectly', and displaying t-shirts printed with the words, 'One tequila, two tequilas, three tequilas, floor!' Apart from updating my blog, there were mundane things we needed to do while we were there in the city. I kept Soozie updated with our travel plans because, after all, the skull was part hers. She was over the moon with the skull's new name.

Shangri-La sometimes gave me 'messages' that seemingly 'sang' in my head. I had devised little rituals to activate it, but kept it well wrapped and hidden from view when travelling. My choice of wrapping materials for any crystal is red cloth, preferably silk, because it protects crystalline energies. My guidance was always very clear: 'This is an ancient sacred object and must be used only with the right intentions, if highly-evolved frequencies are to flow through it.'

I was not going to allow anyone other than myself to take photographs of *Shangri-La*. After regular cleansing with pure water and incense, it was starting to shine much brighter. It was beginning to reflect a higher consciousness, I murmured to myself.

Whenever I'm in Mexico I eventually head off for Chichén Itzá to view carvings there that have deep esoteric meanings. At the *zompantli* or 'skull rack' containing hundreds of carved skulls, day-keeper Hunbatz Men explained in detail how the symbol for a skull represents the number twenty and a long leg-bone represents the number five, so the skull rack is in reality a counting device.

It taught the great relationship that exists between skulls, mathematics and the Milky Way, which has the same numerical value of twenty. 'This is due to the fact that the Milky Way has only made twenty turns in its entire history, *and all this cosmic information is written in our own skull, made of bone, as well as in the crystal skulls.*'

This is an important point: *cosmic information is stored in bone and stone.* Our bodies carry the same harmonic encodements of light, generating the same patterns as rivers, rocks, mountains and trees, making light the primary infrastructure.

Repeatedly I saw the skull as a symbolic representation, showing our head as a gateway between the physical world and the cosmos. The Central American people, by crafting crystal skulls, depictions of skulls, facemasks, ornate symbolic head-dresses, and indeed the giant Olmec heads, exhibited an attention to detail indicating they were very aware of the part the skull plays in interaction between the seen and unseen worlds.

In Chichén's vast ball-court, I wanted to make a closer in-spection of a 'cosmic ballgame player' carved on the wall, who demonstrates these esoteric understandings. The player has six serpents and a flowering tree sprouting from his neck, and a severed skull at his feet represents a ball. But the skull is obviously speaking. Interpretation by Hunbatz Men signifies the growth of an expanded state of consciousness and a flowering of the seven chakra-energy centres, not a real decapitation.

Information received by Lia Scallon when meditating with her crystal skulls was in accord with the information from our shamanic teacher. She wrote:

> The images of death by decapitation in Chichén Itzá and in many other Mayan temple sites do not refer to human sacrifice or physical death. That is a distraction dreamt up by modern day 'experts'! These temples were universities where advanced initiates came to learn the disciplines of spiritual mastery.
>
> The decapitated skulls refer to the mystical death of the lower psychological levels of the self. They depict the ultimate goal of the spiritual warrior, which is to overcome, to die to, the negative and denser emotions of anger, fear, greed, pride and so on, in order that they might achieve 'Crystal Head Consciousness'.
>
> In Toniná, a recently discovered Mayan site, Mayan teachers make it very clear that decapitation of the ego is the path to mystical transformation. Ninety-five per cent of statues in Toniná are decapitated, and a wall in the main temple has a very large skull at its centre, surrounded by flowers. This image of the skull surrounded by flowers, which is also found in Uxmal, represents the joy of the initiate having achieved mystical transformation – pure consciousness and a free spirit without the ties of ego.
>
> It seems clear that, for the ancient Maya, the skull was a dynamic, symbolic representation of a most profound spiritual process. They have left us their teachings on the subject, in a powerful way, on these sacred temple walls.

I thanked Lia for reminding me that images of headless bodies are another historical example connecting us to crystal skulls. They show the decapitation of the ego! It is a modern affliction to refer persistently to ego, a psychological aspect of ourselves unrecognized until the 20th century. In the past the devil sat on our shoulder, but now it is our ego that needs to be reined in, dissolved, or just plain cut off and decapitated.

Some people consider that ego becomes apparent in childhood due to demands to conform and succeed. If that's so, then ego is an addiction. People use it as an excuse. It's an addiction every bit as powerful as smoking or drinking. But we are now adults participating in the greatest adventure since humans first stood upright, we are preparing to evolve and ego has to be released if we are to reach Oneness and unity.

Crystal skulls constantly reflect the need to look within our own skulls for answers. There we will reach clarity. It is there that changes can and must be made if we are to overcome the dual limitations of ego, plus the *karma* imposed upon the human race so long ago to cloud our perceptions and limit dynamic evolution.

The *Chak-muls*

Returning to Chichén Itzá with *Shangri-La*, I was reminded of a longing I had had to spend time in the Temple of the Warriors. Why, I didn't know. Not until I saw the *chak-mul* did the answer pop into my skull. A *chak-mul* is an imposing, larger than human-size stone carving of a semi-recumbent figure, often seen at old Maya ceremonial cities. Reflecting their divine origins, each is resplendent in a royal headdress, together with an Atlantean solar symbol over the heart.

In recent years an excellent copy of a *chak-mul* has been placed on a platform at the top of the steps to the Temple of the Warriors, where warriors once danced. This part of the city is also called the Temple of the Winged Heart. With a flash of insight I realized it was the place for my mission, and its purpose was to link East and West with the *Shangri-La* crystal skull, by honouring the ancient Naga Maya of India and Tibet.

So imagine this particular stone *chak-mul*, who gazes enigmatically over the panorama, guarded by two tall serpent-carved columns. His hands support a small flat altar stone, called an *atlantes*, resting on his abdomen, upon which would have been placed a ritual object. Every 52 years, new fires were lit in each ceremonial city directly from Great Father Sun. Mikhail and I were convinced that, in order to do this, Father Sun's life-giving rays were focused on the *chak-mul*'s altar, through a crystal skull.

I just *knew* that I must place my crystal skull upon this *atlantes* altar. But public access is now denied to many of the monuments in this sacred city, and the Temple of the Warriors was no exception.

I decided to take matters into my own hands. Ducking under a restraining chain, I made a dash up the temple steps and momentarily placed *Shangri-La* upon the altar. Clear guidance immediately flooded into the golden crystal skull forming in my head, directing me to link this Himalayan skull with those ancient Maya ones that had once been honoured upon this altar.

A connection was made. I hadn't come 9,000km to be distracted by the blowing of whistles and the frantic arm-waving of guards out to remove me from the platform of the *chak-mul*. I had something important to accomplish. Everything proceeded well, and my mission was achieved. It worked!

In my own time, and with skull safely stowed again in my rucksack, I got a camera out and snapped a few photos of the view, while the two huge stone serpent columns reared up, seemingly protecting me. But luck was running out and, upon arrival at ground level, I was seized by the guards and led protesting to a site office, whereupon an official confiscated my camera. Saying that I had taken an unauthorized photograph, he removed the film, placing it upon a shelf piled up with dozens of others, refusing to hand it back to me.

Fortunately it seemed that no one had spotted the crystal skull, neither did they know my real reason for visiting the *chak-mul*. Breathing a sigh of relief, still muttering complaints in poor Spanish about my unfair treatment, I returned to the shade of the nearby trees to meet up with Mikhail.

Greater Cycles of Time

My quest to understand more about crystal skulls was about to deepen. All the seeds of wisdom we picked up in the Mayalands were germinating, just like the little soul-seed skulls hanging on the World Tree. Those seeds began their germination as a conversation flowed between Mikhail and I while eating a stack of tasty flat maize tortillas for breakfast.

'Look,' he said, 'What if Time were like this …' pointing at the stack of tortillas.

'Okay, I can imagine our tortillas spiralling off through space and time, never to be seen again,' I laughed.

'No, really, let's be serious for a moment, I want to explain something,' Mikhail insisted, taking a sip of coffee, picking up one tortilla and waving it before me. 'This is equivalent to one Greater or Platonic year of approximately 25,920 years.' (The Platonic Year was devised in classical Greek times by Hipparchus.)

Then, cutting one tortilla into twelve equal segments, Mikhail said, 'Imagine each segment represents one of the twelve astrological signs of the zodiac.'

Pausing to lace the next tortilla with copious *salsa piquante*, he continued, 'The wobble in the Earth's axis takes some 25,920 Earth years to complete a cycle. This axis rotation is the basis upon which the twelve signs of the zodiac are built. Each age (as it is called) lasts approximately 2,160 years, and current belief indicates that humanity is entering an Age of Aquarius.'

'Yes, I am beginning to get the hang of it now', I said. 'I can visualize twelve tortillas stacked on each other. Each one is sub-divided into twelve portions …'

'So, just stay with the concept of Time, represented by Platonic Years, as a lot of tortillas spinning through space. But they are not so much stacked one upon another, but spiralling out, expanding, one from another. Our present Platonic Year is on top of the pile of tortillas.'

'Yes …' I thought out loud. 'Each tortilla must be connected with the next through the spiral. Some astrologers have over-looked the thirteenth sign which moves the circle into a spiralling formation. It's the framework, the structure, or the web upon which the magical impulse of Time sits. Just like Native Americans say, Grandmother Spider sits in Creation spinning her web – and these days the thirteenth sign is called Auriga or Arachne, the spider! So where are we placed now on this stack of tortillas?'

'I'll tell you when I think you've digested your first course!' he joked.

With the tortillas gone and our breakfast and cosmic lesson ended, we left the café, watched by numerous pairs of eyes who had been observing the two gringos doing some very strange things with their tortillas!

The Birth of *Homo Spiritus*

We set off on another of our long car journeys and, at dawn, reached the spectacular waterfalls of Agua Azul near Palenque. Walking up a track into a wilder part of the rainforest towards a

Lacandón village, we sat beneath towering trees, placing the skull *Shangri-La* carefully on the grass beside us. I particularly remember commenting on how her eyes were sparkling in the rising sun and, perhaps, we mused later, with some uncanny anticipation.

Mikhail produced a large bag of delicious ripe yellow mangoes. He began eating them whilst talking. 'Remember our conversation over the stack of tortillas spiralling through space?'

Without waiting for an answer he went on excitedly, 'Look at Time from a different perspective, from way out in space, reflecting a grander cosmological view of humans inhabiting planet Earth.

'Palaeontologists generally agree *Homo sapiens sapiens*, us, modern humans, have lived here for the last 230–250,000 years, a microscopic time-span compared to the 4.5 billion years of the Earth, leaving plenty of room for more ancient civilizations to have existed.

'Remember how we cut our tortillas into twelve pieces, with each piece illustrating an age or influence lasting some 2,160 years, and you asked where we were placed on the stack of twelve tortillas?'

Mikhail began explaining, 'In my calculations, we have reached the ninth Age of Aquarius, the ninth tortilla, in the stack of twelve. Beginning at zero, that equates to some 210,000 years, a time-period shortly after *Homo sapiens sapiens* is said to have evolved. Focus carefully, because the astrological signs divide themselves into four quadrants, Man, Eagle, Lion and Bull, which in spiritual mysticism are known as spiritual, mental, vital and physical, respectively.

'Now is the birthing of the spiritual age of man. The development of humanity has gone through the quadrants eight previous times to reach this spiritual stage. This time-span amounts to approximately 210,000 years, as I have said.'

'Yes, but there is a difference between 210,000 and the 230,000 years that *Homo sapiens* has been around,' I blurted out.

Mikhail smiled knowingly and continued, 'Surely you don't think this is an isolated occurrence of life in the universe? This Earth, this Garden of Eden, is part of a much wider galactic plan. At first humans had to settle into the harsh conditions in different parts of the planet. When these humans were established and considered ready, genetic activation occurred that has led to who and what we are today.'

'Look, Mikhail, I've told you before, I am not so much interested in the past, as in the future. Please explain to me what is happening now to the evolution of humanity.'

Mikhail's eyes clouded over as he picked up *Shangri-La*, then gazed through its eyes, ranging through past and future, and he said, 'The important point I want to emphasize is that *Homo sapiens has been growing through eight complete rounds of the Platonic Year and has now entered the ninth*. We are birthing the evolution of mankind at the beginning of the next cycle in the Age of Aquarius, exactly in the "spiritual" or "man" quadrant. *Those of us incarnate now are present at the evolutionary rebirth of our species.*'

Mikhail replaced *Shangri La* on the grass and I turned my gaze to the dappled pattern of light that was softly falling through the trees. The top of the crystal skull was glowing, indicating how spiritual birth occurs through the Crown chakra.

I continued eagerly, 'Yes, clearly, as you say, the astrological Age of Aquarius that we are entering is the "birthing month". We humans have had eight Platonic Years of "gestation", and now is the fulfilment of that process, "birthing" the ninth age of Aquarian influence. That's why I got the number nine in China during my Tibetan shamanic dream!'

'We have metaphorically been growing within the womb of

Earth Mother for the last 210,000 or so years. At some point in the distant past, crystal skulls were put in place for us to access a continuum of consciousness. They channel a stream of continual light, perhaps the ultraviolet light I mentioned before. Only during this ninth experience of Aquarius can light-transmission codes emerge fully formed. The skulls operate the memory switch that sends light flooding through humanity.'

'Of course,' I exclaimed. 'Light is information, capable of bringing evolutionary consciousness through the crystal skulls into our own skulls and into the future which lies before us. Wow, the crystal skulls switch on the light!'

I paused, collecting my thoughts. 'It is only now, when the human race has completed the "gestation", that we are being given the choice to understand who we really are ... a new humanity can be born! It couldn't have been done at any time in the past, not even just 85 years ago when the first crystal skull to be revealed, the Mitchell-Hedges, was found. Because in those days we didn't fully understand crystals, nor have computers and today's light technology, which unite people in a "global brain".'

Then, looking across to the foaming white falls in the distance, and attuning to the exquisite melodies of the birds' morning chorus, I continued, 'Although I agree with what you are saying about the significance of the Platonic Years, there is also a dynamic way to work with Time on a daily basis, using the traditional Maya *T'zolk'in* sacred calendar. This calendar creates a bond between human and planetary life and the centre of All That Is. It is very complex to understand fully because it was developed by day-keeper astronomers over centuries and centuries of detailed star observation, then interpreted by "jaguar priests" in a way that the people of those days could comprehend.

'Simply put, the basis of this calendar is a twenty-day cycle repeated thirteen times. But the calendar itself is far from simple, because it's an infinitely sophisticated bio-computing device and cosmic timekeeper. By delving deeper into day-keeping we can see how the Maya used their Time science with love and consciousness, because each day has guidance and words for action that align the modern day-keeper with nature, Earth and the foundations of spiritual consciousness.'

I reflected that this calendar is a very good practical tool to help change our perceptions and personal evolvement towards a new consciousness.

'I see what you are getting at,' said Mikhail. 'Of all the Maya calendars, the *T'zolk'in* is prophetic in character, giving windows or gateways in time and space for the evolution of today's humanity. Those humans who foresee and override the galactic waves that we call catastrophic timelines, may, with open heart and mind connections, go safely through to the next level of human evolution. They will have chosen the only sane option, the life-affirming timeline. Some refer to this as "ascension", "co-creation" or "enlightenment" but, whatever we wish to call it, this process will produce a fundamentally different model of human than was living only 500 years ago.'

I picked up my notebook and wrote:

In the process of evolution we will, if we choose the positive timeline presented to us, be poised to co-create an essentially different, peaceful and better world for all. We will move from a conscious state to superconsciousness, achieving this both individually and collectively. This will lead to Oneness, sometimes called unity consciousness.

We will wake up dormant DNA because of activation of the sacred pyramid in the skull, and move through the Crown chakra into a seventh dimension that is simultaneously within and beyond us. We will bring this about by

1. Rare Tibetan crystal skull *Amar*, surrounded by 12 crystal skulls

2. *Amakua* (left), an ancient Tibetan skull, and *Xamuk'u* (right), a ceremonial Mayan skull of citrine

3. Rare Tibetan crystal skull *Amar*

4. *AsKaRa*, a unique and delicately formed articulated jade skeleton from Tibet, used for healing ceremonies

5. Author and husband after ceremony in Mexico, 2006

6. BELOW Temple of the Masks, circa 500 CE, depicting the spirit of the Sun God Kinich Ahau breathing and speaking, Kohunlich sacred city, Mexico

7. Moment of initiation: ball-player's skull speaks within the ball as he achieves cosmic consciousness. Note the six serpents and the tree sprouting from neck. Ball-court, Chichén Itzá

8. BELOW Vision serpent arising during ceremony. Lintel 14, Yaxchilán, Mexico

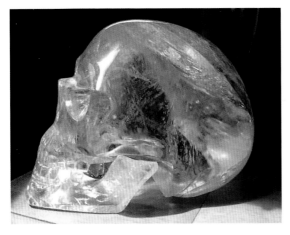

9. *Compassion*, a large quartz healing skull with moveable jaw

10. ABOVE Early Maya carving of Sun God Kinich Ahau

11. Hunbatz Men, daykeeper, Itzá Maya Tradition, Kohunlich, 2006

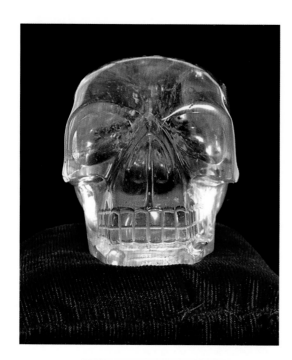

12. *Jomcata Mayab*, an activated modern quartz skull

13. BELOW Red obsidian late-Neolithic shamanic tribal skull from Greater Northeast River District, Inner Mongolia, China

14. Crystal skull guardians presenting their skulls at a Maya initiatory ceremony

15. Star Johnsen-Moser and *Xa-mu-k'u* at Chichén Itzá

16. *Xa-mu-k'u*, life-size quartz skull, at Chichén Itzá

17. The labyrinth – Temple 19, Yaxchilán, Mexico

focusing attention in our own skulls, shifting into *theta* healing states, aided by the message of the crystal skulls. We'll be able to fully access the unimaginably vast quantum field through collective cosmic consciousness.

We will heighten experiences of the Now-moment by accessing converging spiral lines of Time. We'll alter the fundamental resonance of the human complex of mind-body-spirit in such a way that a transition in awareness is made that cannot hold any thoughts about war, destruction, anger or any other negative aspects of life on Earth.

Through evolution of consciousness, the planet and her peoples will enter a new golden age where every thought and action is focused with loving concern rather than profit, honouring the need for fair distribution of sufficient food, water and shelter for all.

We will halt the extinction of endangered animal and plant species, allowing a balanced biodiversity to flourish, and this will result in climate change and natural disasters no longer being seen as problematic areas.

We have a parallel challenge, that of personal and group consciousness transformation and transformation of our societies and environments. Neither one is achievable on its own – they are as inseparable as our two hands.

'Mikhail, I remember you once saying that our brain structure hasn't substantially changed since Neolithic times. Yet its potential to receive and respond to information and other external stimuli has expanded dramatically. Today, many of us are becoming increasingly aware of being part of a global brain, which was unthinkable to Neolithic man.'

'So just where do you think we are now heading, in evolutionary terms?'

'Dormant DNA can be "switched on" under certain circumstances, but even with advanced human genome research we may never know scientifically what is causing the activation. From the perspective of evolution, all that is needed is for the hidden pieces of the human puzzle to fall into place. Or, put another way, remember those cosmic tortillas spiralling through space?'

'How could I forget them? They were all connected in a spiral by the spider's web, or the matrix of Creation. It guided them in their spiralling orbit further and further out into deepest space.' Mikhail's voice rose with excitement. 'During the last part of our present cycle of 25,920 years, we have evolved exponentially.'

'You only have to look at the civilizations that have risen and fallen, culminating with our own. It has all been a trial for something really big that is about to happen. Now we are in Aquarius and we have been prepared for a great leap in evolution. A pivotal point is arising.'

He stressed, '*We must decide between two timelines: the annihilation and disaster timeline or the one that will give us a positive outcome.* We must do this on both a personal and a collective level. The point at which we are poised concerns time and space since our current location in the cosmos is critical for sustaining life. Within our solar system Earth is the chosen planet suitable for this development, because only on Earth is the "garden" ready for the next stage of human super-life to grow.

'At the present time we don't know whether conditions for simple or more advanced life exist elsewhere. Great astronomers such as Carl Sagan initiated a search for signs of life in the cosmos. He was even instrumental in sending a message plaque about our planet into deep space, but mainstream science continues to state there is no other planet or moon able to support human life as we know it.'

I held my head in my hands as the golden crystal skull in my innerscape clarified how we humans are liable for the quality of our future life. Every one of us is capable of contributing to an all-encompassing answer to the world's problems. They won't all be solved if we immediately stop using excessive amounts of oil or throw out seeds engineered with terminator genes, but it will be a start.

More importantly, changes will continue to come about through grassroots initiatives, instead of from the top down. They will percolate through our tired-out systems and archaic rules like a cup of freshly brewed coffee. The cream on top will be a lessening of mental stress, coupled with a sugaring of personal acts of kindness. Just like the luscious aroma of hot coffee, these changes will draw in more and more people who, each in their own ways, will initiate positive optimistic transformation of self and society.

The Agua Azul waterfalls were becoming busier, as noisy flocks of tourists replaced the early morning birdsong. I needed some strong coffee and breakfast to 'ground' myself! *Shangri-La* was also telling me it was time to move on. The link with the golden crystal skull in my head was broken and I came back to normality with a clear idea of what was to happen next.

More and more people were walking past us. The little village settlement was slowly awakening and Lacandón men in their distinctive loose white tunics were going about their simple daily lives, as they had done for millennia. (Recently I've heard that a crystal skull has been presented to them for use in traditional ceremonies.) It was time to go and find that coffee!

I picked up *Shangri-La*, smiled at Mikhail and scooped up a little of the river water to refresh myself and splash upon the skull, whilst mentally thanking it for our insights. I looked across at the foaming waters rushing through the falls of Agua Azul, marvelling at nature's ability to demonstrate exactly how to flow and transform, even though its power is unstoppable.

I kept marvelling at the perfection of this greater plan. We humans, at this stage of our development, are poised on the edge of Time – beyond that edge is the Great Mystery. Carl Sagan commented, 'Somewhere, something incredible is waiting to be known.' This is the time that humanity has been waiting for. We are beginning to *remember* how to use our energy wisely to evolve. We are at the point of co-creation.

We can do it. We can use our personal energy to nourish the necessary intelligence that can contribute to the advancement of collective consciousness within humanity on Earth – called superconsciousness.

We can use our individual enlightened intelligence to assemble the essence of a truly spiritual human by linking heart and head, sending out a transcendent beam of illumination through the top of our skulls. We can use it to birth this co-creation.

Crystal skulls are here now. *We are remembering* where and when to access this process – this birthing – in our own skulls!

·

CHAPTER EIGHT

The Nine Lords of Time

I had one other encounter with Don Pablo and talking stones.
One day, after he had done some work on the camp kitchen, I
found a clear glass marble in the area. Thinking it belonged to
Don Pablo and that it was one of his saso'ob, the 'lights' he
used when focusing spiritual forces, I took it next door to him
that evening. He took the marble and inspected it carefully.
'Yes,' he said finally, 'This is a stone of light.' Then he smiled.
'However, it won't speak until it has been soaked in maize gruel,
sak-a, and then it will only speak Maya.'

– 'TALKING STONES', FROM *MAYA COSMOS* BY **DAVID FREIDEL**,
LINDA SCHELE AND **JOY PARKER**

We were off to Guatemala. On the short flight I reclined in
my seat, turning over in my mind just how significant it
had become not only to understand, but also to work more closely
with my higher faculties of perception as humanity begins the
rebirth process. The sacred pyramid in my skull was calling for
my full attention.

I felt this would be easier to achieve in the ancient cities. It would help me understand everything that a friend, Star Johnsen-Moser, was about to tell me of her long experiences with crystal skulls. It had become clear that, if I were to progress further into their mysteries, I must daily access the truths embodied in the Maya *T'zolk'in* calendar.

So I was consistently taking heed of auspicious days, following guidance received from ancestral day-keepers. Despite this, I chose the wrong day for travel and, after our flight, we found ourselves trapped at a roadblock by angry gun-wielding *campesinos* (villagers).

The Nine Lords of Time

The noise of the plane's engines was lulling me to sleep, so in order to keep awake I thought again about the importance of number nine. I had been told to remember it when we were in China, and I had a strong sense of a need to reflect on the Nine Lords of Time.

I'd heard about an interesting inscription on a time-worn monument from Tortuguero in Mexico, dated to around 670 CE. The translation looks rather strange because the original stone is damaged, but this doesn't detract from its importance as a major prophetic source. This is the translation, proposed by experts, and it appears to predict that nine cosmic forces or 'support gods' are to manifest *within our current era*, at the end of the Thirteenth *Baktun* (on 21st December 2012):

The Thirteenth Baktun will be finished on 4 *Ajaw*, the Third of *Uniiw* (*K'ank'in*). (?) will occur (it will be) the descent of the Nine Support Gods to the (?).

Hmm, nine ..., I thought. *Nine, the number of aspiration and wisdom.* There is something gathering around this mystery. I had already thought a lot about different aspects of it.

There was the predicted descent of the Nine Support Gods or cosmic forces, as carved on the Tortuguero monument. Then there are the Nine Lords of Time, coming from traditional Maya teaching. There are the nine underworlds and thirteen heavens, another traditional Maya teaching, and the nine evolutionary levels, in which we are now peaking at the apex of a pyramid shape comprising the levels of evolution on Earth.

Then there are the nine dimensions of conscious evolvement (based on Buddhist teachings) beyond which a human is unable to go. There are nine rounds of the Platonic Year during which modern human develops, and now we are entering the astrological Age of Aquarius for the ninth time in the ninth Platonic Year, awaiting a birth-type event.

I reviewed the theories of a Maya researcher and author, Dr Carl Calleman, concerning nine evolutionary levels through which Earth has transitioned since the beginning of time. He suggests there is overwhelming evidence that the Mayan calendar describes sequential shifts in consciousness, which will imminently begin to be experienced at high frequencies. Mentioning the Tortuguero inscription, he said:

> On my own part I think that we are approaching something much more profound than just a point in a cycle that again will be repeated. The only Mayan inscription from ancient times, the Tortuguero monument, which describes the end of their calendar, says that nine cosmic forces will then manifest.

> Empirically, there is also overwhelming evidence from

modern research that we are approaching a point in time when nine evolutionary levels (so called underworlds) of the cosmic plan are simultaneously going to be completed.

This would imply that we are approaching not another cycle or another shift, but the end to all shifts, which have been driving evolution since the beginning of the universe. Such an end to all shifts could conceivably provide the basis for a harmonious eternal peace on Earth.

So here I had chanced upon a tangible connection between the nine cosmic forces, nine evolutionary levels and the Nine Lords of Time I had first discovered at Palenque.

I was feeling sleepy and my head was reeling as, within myself, I saw the great and powerful Lords of Time, each in their own energy dimension and each holding a crystal skull. What this was like in reality is pretty hard to describe. But it was a revelation to see how a simple myth like this has a sacred origin, if we expand it from an everyday to a quantum universe concept.

The Lords of Time were swirling backwards and forwards around me in a dreamtime state from which I didn't want to wake. They were sitting, or perhaps floating, there right before my eyes within the unfolding timelines. Quantum thought-implants were placed in my head. Each Lord had been responsible for a level of Earth's development since the beginning of Time. They told me that their Mayan name was *Bolon Tiku*. It became quite a revelation. What I was being shown was so vast that I suddenly pulled out of dreamtime – my rational mind couldn't take it anymore! I felt confused and dizzy.

Once the quantum thought implants became active within my head, in a kind of 're-booting process', the significance of the thirteen skulls came into focus. The Nine Lords each held a skull, which represented each level of Earth's development.

The additional four skulls were keepers of the spiritual aspects pertaining to our familiar four dimensions.

I now knew the importance of the Tortuguero carving. I was in awe at the prophetic abilities of the calendar-keepers of old. Their hearts beat to a different cosmic rhythm, hailing from a tradition when great cosmic knowledge was uncluttered by the complexities of modern life. Surging within them was wisdom that could even illuminate generations to come, because they predicted the reincarnated masters will soon return to Earth.

This prediction is echoed by *hau'k'in* Hunbatz Men of the Itzá Maya tradition: 'Reincarnated masters will be able to travel like the wind, descend like the rain, give warmth like fire and teach like Mother Earth.' He tells us that they will come from many places in the cosmos, they will be of many colours and speak of things difficult to understand. All of them will communicate a profound initiatory message, which is to continue through the cycles of this millennium, to enlighten the initiates of the future in an age of peace.

Finally too, the singing aspect that set these thirteen skulls aside from all others was revealed to me. If they really were extra-terrestrial in origin, as I'd seen during hypnosis, the property of 'singing' needs to be understood because quartz originating from other parts of the galaxy has additional qualities within it, linking to communication from intelligent silica-based life-forms.

We picked up our bags, ready to leave the plane, and I was amazed to see a newspaper that had been left by a passenger. It contained an article about growing super-crystals in the International Space Station. I was trying to work out the significance of this and, while waiting for the exit door to open, I said to Mikhail, 'Now I know humanity's rebirth is connected with the descent of the Nine Gods or, as I prefer to say, the Nine Lords of Time.'

Mikhail answered, 'It's clear, as you say, the Nine Lords of

Time have influenced different developmental epochs of Earth and humanity. Now they are returning. The ancient Maya left a message for us at Tortuguero so that we would understand the cosmic influences of this pivotal point in time and human evolution, which *hau'k'in* wisdom has confirmed.'

'Yes. The nine influences, represented by the Nine Lords of Time, are an intrinsic part of Earth and human spiritual evolution. A skull was assigned to each of the Nine Lords. And these nine, together with the dimensions of length, breadth, depth and time, make up that mysterious number thirteen. It all confirms my belief that humanity's evolutionary leap of superconsciousness through Time into the dimensions beyond is symbolized by the thirteen crystal skulls.'

Auspicious Days

Arriving in Guatemala City, I realized this was the appointed day for a coordinated crystal skull meditation through my Skullmeet blog site. Also, I still had a lot more to understand about the thirteen skulls. Mikhail went out to buy some food and arrange car hire, and I remained alone in our simple room for the meditation.

Perhaps I was feeling jetlagged but, whatever it was, I couldn't settle down. A disruptive energy seemed to be disturbing me as I tried to 'tune in' at the appropriate time with *Shangri-La*, my Himalayan skull. All I was getting was a feeling of apprehension, as if something momentous and frightening was about to happen. *How much better*, I thought, *if we could have made it all the way to beautiful Antigua instead of this city, with its dangerous reputation.* Beneath my window, truck fumes belched out in dense choking clouds, and sounds of the nearby bus station seemed raucous and threatening. In the room the air was heavy and stifling.

I adjusted my position, took three deep breaths and began the meditation again. A sudden noise at the window disturbed me. I jolted out of my meditation as a figure jumped down from the balcony outside and ran off quickly in the street below, dodging the fast-moving mass of cars and old trucks. One moment he was there and in the next gone.

Obviously the man thought we had both left the rundown hotel and was about to enter our room. There I was, holding on to the skull and shaking with fright. Not a good start to our Guatemalan travels.

I ran down to the front desk. The young woman there, painting her fingernails purple, the same colour as her toes, was nonchalant in her reaction. 'Dios Mío,' she exclaimed, gesticulating in the direction of the market, indicating that I would find La Madre and Los Santos there – apparently these saints would help me.

Crossing over to the market I recognized the Virgin of Guadaloupe and Santo Hermano Pedro, known as Saint Francis of the Americas, gracing many market stalls. People here hold fast to religious customs, so these stalls do a great trade. Finding a plastic-covered pendant of the Virgin, the best of a bad selection of objects, I settled on her and hoped that the locals would be convinced of her protective efficacy – even if I wasn't!

The next day, being day 7 *Ee* (7 *Eb* in Yucatec Maya), was an auspicious day on which to travel, so we set off for Antigua. Thinking that we would take the long scenic route rather than the main road, we loaded our cases into the car. Getting into the passenger seat, I said, 'Where's my day-sack?'

'I put it behind your seat.'

'No, it isn't there.'

'It must be!'

Shangri-la the skull was in the day-sack, carefully wrapped in a piece of red woven Guatemalan material. It had disappeared. That thief, who had been at the window the day before, must have been hanging around wanting to pick up anything he could – hoping for money or cameras, perhaps.

The next five hours were spent at the police station, reporting our loss. Quite an experience! Just how do you explain in Spanish that you are telling them about a *crystal* skull, and not even a real one? Our interviewers' expressions alternated between frustration, amusement and a kind of 'these gringos are nutters'.

There was nothing we could do but continue with our journey. But things still weren't going well. We hadn't driven more than a few kilometres out of the city into the mountainous countryside when, rounding a bend, we were halted by a large tree trunk lying across the road. Screeching to a halt, we saw a crowd of villagers sitting on a dry mud bank silently watching us. One young man holding a shotgun swaggered over, putting out his hand.

'Dollars,' he said. 'Pay dollars.' He held up his fingers. 'Pay five, five hundred.' This was becoming one hell of a day, hardly auspicious.

'What shall we do, Mikhail?'

'Well we haven't got $500 on us,' he said.

'We're not rich tourists,' I tried to explain in my poor Spanish.

The young man just shrugged, turned away and sat down, gun pointing toward us. This was obviously going to turn into a waiting game. We returned to the car and sat down too.

'The villagers don't look scary,' I said to Mikhail. 'I think they only want a bit of money. There's a lot of hardship around here. They look as though they haven't got two pennies to rub together. Let's sit it out.'

We waited. It got hotter and hotter in the car. They sat silently staring at us. We didn't eye them too much. A few of the men and boys sat on the tree trunk, smoking and chattering. This was going to take a long time. Then I had an idea.

I took out one of the small quartz healing crystals I always carry with me and tied my red ceremonial headband around my forehead. Striding into the centre of the road I knelt down in the dust, holding the virgin pendant in one hand and the crystal in the other. I started waving my arms around and calling up all the Catholic saints and Mayan deities I could remember, speaking in English but adding all their names together in one long litany. The guys on the log in front of me started to look apprehensive.

'*Una brujera rubia* – a blonde witch,' they whispered amongst themselves. They were now looking agitated. One or two got up and sauntered to the far side of the road. Suddenly the chains attached to the tree roadblock tightened, and the atmosphere tightened too.

I jumped back into the car. Mikhail took $100 from his pocket and pushed it into the young man's hand. The tree was pulled back. We were free!

Continuing on, I reflected that I felt safer with the villagers at the roadblock than I would have done if heavily armed patrols of soldiers had turned up – soldiers had a dubious reputation. However, I now had time to think about the stolen skull. An un-expected despair hung around my head. I really felt the loss. It was as if a friend was missing. But there was nothing I could do.

I was also becoming increasingly agitated, wanting to get back to civilization and find an internet café. I had a lot to put on my blog.

'It almost seems an obsession with you', Mikhail commented. But what we found two days later, when we drove around Lake Atitlan, was not the internet but another form of communication from a life-sized being called Maximom.

Strange Encounters

It was 'the day of the shaman and the jaguar' called 9 *I'x* (9 *Ix*) in the sacred calendar. Walking along a dusty track in a village on the shores of Lake Atitlan, we were called by a boy of about ten. '*Ven aqui, ven aqui!* – come here, come here!' He led us to an old house. On our travels we had become used to strange encounters, and this was such an occasion. We were reverently ushered into a dark room. Liquid pools of light from candles illuminated a shrine, not to one of the Maya gods or to the Virgin of Guadalupe, but to a strangely dressed effigy.

'It's Maximom,' I whispered to Mikhail. 'He's regarded as a kind of saint that was introduced by local people around the time of the Spanish conquest. That's why he's wearing those old-fashioned clothes.'

'Lucky him, he's smoking a cigar too,' observed Mikhail as Maximom's keeper, a thin old man, lit one up and stuck it in the effigy's mouth.

I glanced around, my eyes beginning to adjust to the darkness, in contrast to the bright sun outside. 'Mikhail, look, there's an altar to the Virgin as well.' I pointed to a flower-covered *ofrenda*. 'She's peaceful and beautiful. Quite the opposite to Maximom, who seems a strange old character.'

The boy insisted that we sit on two low stools in front of Maximom. Feeling a bit scared, I didn't have the urge to do so. The energy was oppressive and inexplicably dense. I had the feeling that, bound up with this effigy, was all the *karma*, the horror, that the Conquistadors had unleashed upon the Maya. I just wanted to get outside and breathe fresh air. It was the closest I have ever been to a panic attack – my breath was becoming laboured.

Mikhail didn't even notice. He had gone off into a deep meditation, his head dropping to his chest – I wasn't going to get any help from him. I couldn't draw my eyes away from Maximom's painted eyes. They had turned translucent, looking almost alive.

Although in normal circumstances I would have known better, I sensed my unconscious mind was being psychically attacked. Someone or something was trying to read my mind. It felt like claws holding on to me. They were stabbing into my brain. I simply wanted to escape. Mentally I tried to pull away. Holding on tightly to my plastic pendant of the Virgin, I got up to leave. This seemed to have the desired effect. My focus switched from the hypnotic pull of Maximom to the sweet, flower-bedecked Virgin in the opposite corner of the dark room. Mikhail stirred, my breathing stabilized and I tugged at his elbow to get him out of the place.

'This is more than I want to deal with today,' I implored Mikhail. 'Let's go for a swim in the lake. I must wash these bad energies away.'

After a cooling bathe, we finally got to an internet café. When I logged on to Skullmeet, it occurred to me that someone was following my blog and following me! It wasn't identity theft, but something much more invasive. Mikhail had been right. I was convinced 'they' were trying to read my mind, and I hadn't even realized it until I had sat in that room with weird old Maximom.

The forces of darkness can be sinister and insidious when one is caught unawares and unprepared. They slide into our consciousness unannounced. Some call it madness, others just obsession, others a 'holy' crusade. Sometimes they manifest full-blown as Nazi interrogators or suicide bombers. Sometimes they take the form of little doubts prompted by an uncaring remark, or of friends suddenly stabbing you in the back, spreading lies or half-truths. I had begun to get some nasty responses to my blog, such as, 'Hi bitch, what gutter did you crawl out of?' And others too pornographic to mention.

Over the last hundred years or so some crystal skulls had been put to negative and destructive use. There is even a black one called the Nazi skull. Others are reputed to be held by secret societies and used with malign intent. How amazing that objects of such beauty could be misused by anyone, but even the awesome Mitchell-Hedges skull was once called the Skull of Doom. Some people can't bear to look at the skulls at all, calling them 'creepy'.

My blog was also attracting invasive marketing attention. Constant unsuitable advertisements were coming through, despite my computer software being regularly upgraded to eliminate such things. Then, even some of my blog 'friends' were not who they seemed to be.

Earlier, I had announced my new crystal skull talk – it was to be in three months' time. The announcement went out on Skull-meet, but the pictures of beautiful crystal skulls I attached to it were then overlaid with nasty comments. It didn't occur when most people logged on to the blog – it happened only with some computers, belonging to my most trusted lightworker friends. What was happening? My thoughts flashed back to the ALTA prediction abilities that Karl had talked about, and to hackers sitting in some slum in Asia trying to access my bank account – or worse!

I needed to ask a trusted expert to sort it out and Karl was the person. 'Perhaps it's a selective virus?' I asked him. 'No, it's not that easy to fix. It looks like a new cosmic wormhole,' he replied, using his jargon. 'If it's a black hole we'll never eradicate it,' he said pessimistically. 'Something or someone is logging in to the cosmic energy-field and causing all kinds of electromagnetic anomalies. These are showing up on computers owned by highly sensitive people.' Karl suddenly grinned at the thought of the challenge and I was left wondering whether or not he was in a fantasy world.

This was all very well, but I *needed* my computer and blog – or so I thought at the time. As it happened, it wasn't just paranoia. Something or someone *was* following my every move. They were watching me when I travelled, keeping tabs on me. Was I moving too close to the truth about the skulls? Moving too far into the light? In my innocence I had become a threat.

I was really remembering. *I was even remembering without the aid of my crystal skull.* I began to concentrate much more upon the mysteries of Time and the coming age of transformation. After all, even without *Shangri-La* I could still call upon the golden crystal skull in my head. As I found when healing with crystals, I really don't need a crystal skull to be there physically – I only have to channel the appropriate frequency. Nevertheless, *Shangri-La* was still sorely missed.

Every so often I telephoned the police station in Guatemala City to see if the skull had been recovered. Not very likely, but I kept telling myself that the thief wouldn't really be interested in keeping such an object. One morning over breakfast, I was feeling sad about it, and even Mikhail's comic efforts at describing flying tortillas spiralling through space didn't lift my mood!

I decided to log on again to Skullmeet, to see what was happening. There was information posted about more crystal skulls being revealed, a huge quartz skull called *Einstein*, a large crystal buffalo skull and a curious humanoid bone skull named the *Starchild*, with distinctly extraterrestrial features.

Max and a Cosmic Language

I didn't want too many distractions at this stage of my research, so I put intrigue about the *Starchild* behind me. A very experienced crystal skull guardian, Star Johnsen-Moser, a Solar Initiate and director of the Cahokia Mysteries School for Cosmic Education, was next to answer my questions. She is a channel and spiritual healer who has encountered many crystal skulls, coming to understand them from an experiential standpoint, communicated through feelings rather than through intellect. One skull she worked with regularly was the beautiful and famous quartz skull *Max*, kept in the USA under the guardianship of JoAnn Parkes.

I had asked Star, 'In what ways are crystal skulls connected with the evolution of spiritual consciousness?'

Every crystal skull I have worked with over 23 years has assisted me in connecting with ever-deepening levels of Oneness which, in my understanding, is the beginning and end of spiritual consciousness. The Creation was born out of Oneness, and as we evolve we make a full circle as we return to Oneness.

In this profound spiritual work we are reconnecting and re-uniting with many aspects of our true Self, from which we became disconnected. That is really what it's about now. It is an awakening within you as to who you are as a multidimensional soul.

What does it mean to become a perfect master? It is my understanding that when one becomes fully awakened and reconnected, one is aware of one's existence in all dimensions, on all levels of being, simultaneously.

So this means that all of the spiritual work that we are doing with our crystal skulls is being recorded for future generations to access, just as we are accessing now what has been programmed into the ancient crystal skulls by the Old Ones. *We are the Old Ones of the future.*

Difficult as it was to understand everything that Star shared without having experienced it, her words made much more sense than obscure threats from the internet. I decided to get on with my life, with more book research, and to find out where the crystal skulls can take us.

A curious rapport, a feeling of oneness was deepening within me whenever a crystal skull guardian shared profound insights. Carl Sagan, the astronomer, once wrote, 'For small creatures such as we, the vastness is bearable only through love'. It was a sentiment with which I completely resonated.

Synergy

Many crystal skulls have fascinating stories attached to them, but some I am not at liberty to reveal. However, one with an enthralling story about its origins is *Synergy*. This quartz skull weighs in at a hefty 15.5lbs. It is under the present guardianship of Sherry Whitfield. The story goes that it was kept by a Catholic nun who lived in late-1600s Peru. She called the skull 'An inheritance from a lost civilization' and, when she died, it was passed on to a Peruvian man and his son.

The skull was handed down through their family, who safeguarded it until the 'right' person came along. Apparently the nun had said, 'Your heart will know the right person.' Eventually it was passed to a businessman named George. In 2001 George was on a business trip to the USA and felt compelled to give it to a woman, Sherry Whitfield, whom he hardly knew. Sherry's and *Synergy*'s work together deepened over the years. Now it is rooted in building a group vibration that encompasses compassion, acceptance and an ever-increasing ability to give and receive love.

There was a further twist to this story, when an Aboriginal man living on an island near Australia saw a photograph of *Synergy*. He was so struck with it that he undertook a long journey to see the crystal skull. There was instant recognition of the skull. When he got back to his island, he presented a small skull that had been with *Synergy*, with more photographs, to his chief. The members of the tribe were overjoyed. They recalled how, generations before, their ancestors had been guardians of *Synergy*, but they were guided to send it across the ocean in a small boat that landed in Hawaii and then went on to South America.

Even stranger, to this day the tribe reveres skulls and has several old crystal skulls in its possession. They were adamant that they did not carve them but that they came originally from the lost continent of Lemuria or Mu, known as the Motherland.

CHAPTER NINE

·

The Visionaries

We stand now where two roads diverge. The road we have long
been travelling is deceptively easy, a smooth superhighway on
which we progress with great speed, but at its end lies disaster.
The other fork of the road – the one less travelled by – offers our
last, our only chance to reach a destination that assures the
preservation of the Earth.

– **RACHEL CARSON** (1907–64), ZOOLOGIST AND
A FOUNDER OF THE ENVIRONMENTAL MOVEMENT

Signs are coming into human consciousness directing us
toward a profound change of consciousness – the evolvement
of a new type of human – and crystal skulls play a key part in this
process if their presence is invoked.

One of my Maya teachers, respected elder Don Alejandro
Cirillo Oxlaj Perez, said this during a visit to Tikal, Guatemala: 'It
is important that cosmic knowledge be recorded and stored for
future generations, in such a way as to survive the coming massive
Earth changes that are prophesied as we near Zero Point on the

Mayan Calendar' – referring to 2012. 'And what better way to record this information than in a crystal skull?'

The Vision of a Crystal Skull Guardian

I posed one of my questions to healer Joanne Van Wijgerden, a crystal skull guardian and healer: 'In what ways are the skulls connected with the evolution of spiritual consciousness?' She answered:

Skulls are connected with evolution both on an individual level and on a collective level. There is general guidance that we don't abuse the sacred information for our own selves, like we did in Atlantis, and the more you are heart-centred as an individual or as a collective, the more information the skulls will share. When my fields open up, the fields of my skull open up to an even bigger extent. We humans form a network to the extent that we are heart-centred, and so do the crystal skulls. They have no problems working together and sharing their knowledge, as they have no ego to overcome.

In my background as a healer, I honour all native sources of healing and shamanism all over the world. The more I explore this, the more I realize that they all share the same source and same sacred knowledge. So to me it is completely natural that the old skulls share the same information, though we might have easier access to either one form or another. Or the codes might differ from the Himalayan and the Central American old skulls.

It fills me with awe to realize that the form of a skull, like the human being, contains extended fields of information about the universe, our galactic roots, our history beyond any history book, and about healing possibilities we are hardly touching yet. It does give an idea about the potential · of our human race. But this may take a while in three-dimensional years.

Changing Human Consciousness

Professor Ervin Laszlo, twice nominated for the Nobel Peace Prize, is the founder and president of the Club of Budapest. He is an interdisciplinary scientist, philosopher and author of 83 books.

His work demonstrates how cutting-edge science is investigating and confirming knowledge once confined to areas of mystic interpretation. He highlights a shift away from an anthropocentric focus to the multidimensional world and a unifying quantum field – the Akashic Field. One of his observations, in his book *Quantum Shift in the Global Brain*, reads as follows:

> We have arrived at a historic bifurcation, at the critical -phase of the global macro-shift. While we now find ourselves on a descending path toward growing social, political, and environmental crises, we could also enter on an ascending path leading to a system of social, economic and political organization that is peaceful and capable of ensuring sustainability for human communities and the planetary environment. The choice is open, and making it depends on our values, beliefs and vision and – as we shall see – on our ethic.

His expression 'macro-shift' means that we must make constructive change in and around ourselves at a personal level or become complicit in the ultimate breakdown of our society. Mixing a unique blend of environmental truths with economic forecasts, he shows the need to honour a new vision by discarding outdated beliefs, both individual and collective, for a new paradigm and planetary ethic.

Laszlo explains the significance of Native American cultures, including the Hopi, Maya and Cherokee, who speak from a position of sensing a conscious connection with Mother Earth and who say we are about to enter an age of transformation. What the outcome will be, we do not yet know. But at an individual level, if the urgency is understood and a significant number of people awaken to ethical guidance, we may yet collectively make a quantum shift in the global brain and achieve evolved consciousness.

'Global brain' (Lazlo's term) refers to the great awakening happening to people worldwide as they champion cultures of peace and care for the environment. Superconsciousness, Gebser's integral state of mind, the Akashic Field, a unified field, hyperspace, holofield, implicate order, Oneness and unity are all way-markers in this great adventure.

The shift in consciousness is already taking place among innumerable positive initiatives worldwide, where small groups of people are working on the ascending path that Laszlo refers to. Good initiatives such as these rarely make headline news. Here are a few examples.

In the Brazilian Amazon, rainforest management projects such as the Amazon John project empower local people to protect the ethno-botany of the region. In the Straits of Gibraltar a team takes tourists on dolphin watches, using the fees generated to fund ongoing research to preserve cetaceans. There is a move to ban toxic pesticides worldwide, instead of just doing this in Europe and North America while offloading stocks to less-developed countries.

Survival International has developed assisted protection for uncontacted tribal people, and set up guidelines to preserve their environment. Grassroots movements such as Transition Towns groups help local communities improve their resilience and adaptability to peak-oil and climate change.

The priority of the World Wisdom Council (WWC) is 'The formation of networks, partnerships, and collaborations in the interest of mobilizing the forces required for constructive transformation on a global scale'. Finally, the World Social Forum, which acts as a contrasting mirror to the World Economic Forum that meets annually in Davos, brings together social and ethical groups and movements worldwide.

Evolution of Consciousness

Jean Gebser (1905–73), a visionary philosopher, gave some answers to the question of evolution of consciousness. In *The Ever-present Origin* he proposed five states of consciousness, each one a profoundly different understanding of time and space. He called them the *archaic* structure, the *magic* structure, the *mythical* structure, the *mental* structure and the *integral* structure.

The mental is our present stage, with the previous three being ascribed to the quality of our consciousness in previous periods in history. Moving beyond these four states leads us into Gebser's *integral* state of unified consciousness. In this book I refer to this as *superconsciousness*.

Describing the most recent changes to humanity, Gebser wrote, 'In dividing itself from its past, the mental mind abandoned the ambivalent and ambiguous polarities that characterized the mythic world, based on its projections of the soul and psyche, for duality, a "diminished and mentalized form" of thought, separating matter and mind, rationality and intuition, organic and inorganic.'

His theory was concerned with the transition of human consciousness, explaining that transitions are not continuous mutations, but sometimes massive leaps into the unknown, involving *structural changes in mind and body*. Starting from the time when the earliest humans walked the Earth, there were a number of times when human minds and bodies went through changes. Gebser identified them sequentially in the form of the different levels mentioned above.

Gebser concluded that humanity has almost reached the limits of the mental structure. As we collectively release the traumas of war and conflict, individuals mutate from the mental structure to the integral, whilst at the same time each individual act has an effect upon the whole, so that eventually *all human consciousness integrates*. At that point, the integral structure of consciousness is achieved.

This concept is similar to the unifying principles highlighted by contemporary visionary researchers such as biochemist Rupert Sheldrake, physicist David Bohm, neurophysiologist Karl Pribram and psychiatrist David Hawkins. It is also not so far removed from the idea of a critical mass of 144,000 enlightened beings, who will lead humanity into a new way of being, spoken of by Hopi Nation elders in the USA.

Gebser offered us a challenge: 'Are we willing to settle into the comfort of our daily life or to take on the process of change?' He also urged us to realize that *we are what we think*.

This has a direct bearing on the ability to heighten our consciousness – actually to *envision* a fairer world that in some sense we co-create. Within mainstream science a new paradigm has evolved, suggesting that the world we believe to be solid and physical is actually a holographic projection from a higher dimension of pure consciousness. The skill is to access it from any time and any place. The frontiers of science are finally catching up with what spiritual teachers have told us for thousands of years – we are not separate and we are entangled in and part of an infinite continuum which encompasses everything.

To explain this, let me describe how a hologram is a 3D image projected into space using a laser. The characteristic of a hypothetically perfect hologram is that all of its content is contained in any finite part of itself, but at lower resolution. This led to ideas of a holographic universe, now expanded upon by a growing number of scientists.

This is pertinent to what people working with crystal skulls say about their experiences. The skulls can project holographic images within their cranium, rather as a magician's crystal ball was once said to produce pictures. As we change and grow in our understandings of a limitless universe, we would be wise to be open to the metaphysics of paranormal and mystical experiences.

We can talk about and rationalize groundbreaking concepts as much as we like, but really we need to *experience* them. Just how can we do that authentically? Our innate abilities to tune in like a radio to different interpenetrating but distinct frequency fields accounts for all kinds of paranormal phenomena, connected with slips in time which occur when we move from one frequency or dimension to another.

Such phenomena include seeing apparitions and ghosts, precognition, religious revelations, spontaneous enlightenment, channelling, enhanced feelings of connection with a higher force during meditation, prophetic dreams, hypnosis, out-of-body or near-death experiences, distant healing, dowsing, drug-stimulated encounters, shamanic journeys and, in the growing child, daydreaming. In the everyday world there is some misunderstanding, mislabelling and mistreatment of people exhibiting these abilities.

Earth's Resonance as a Tuning-Fork for Life

The Schumann Frequency is a fluctuating electromagnetic energy in the space between the surface of the Earth and the ionosphere. It was first discovered in 1954 by a German physicist, W O Schumann, and then linked to human brainwave frequencies by Ankermüller and König. The fundamental frequency of the Earth is 7.83 cycles per second, the same as alpha brainwave levels (evident during light meditation and sleep), and it has implications for the evolution of human life.

So far as is known, the Schumann Frequency is primarily governed by electrical storms, volcanoes and sunspot activity. Some researchers suggest that the 7.83 fundamental frequency, or the resonances to it, is rising. Others, such as Dr W Ludwig, state that mammalian life is dependent upon this spectrum of electromagnetic fields because this frequency range within our atmosphere stores resonant patterns of information, bridging the solar system and brain by means of our DNA.

Life on Earth has evolved so far in balance with the 'tuning-fork' of life – the Schumann Frequency. Apparently nuclear devices have already perforated the ionosphere that acts as a protective shield around the Earth. What could we expect if severe climate changes occur or a weapon such as HAARP made dramatic alterations to it?

Sri Kalki Bhagavan, founder of the Oneness Movement and Golden Age Foundation, India, talks of huge changes to the Earth in the coming years, principally determined by an increase in the strength of the Schumann frequency. Kalki hypothesizes that if it rose to 13 cycles per second, the Earth's inner iron core would stop rotating. This would cause the magnetic field to collapse, with catastrophic consequences to all manner of global systems. We would be disorientated, with disruption to our brainwave functions, on an environmentally barren wasteland of a planet.

Whilst this appears to be a dire situation, Kalki goes on to link our minds to all *karma*, which he believes is stored in the Earth's magnetic field. He says that, with the field at zero for a few days, our *karma* would be gone. To those seeking enlightenment, it would be an apposite emerging moment for a new humanity and the dawn of a golden age.

These radical ideas fascinated me, especially when doctor David Hamilton MD says in his book *How Your Mind Can Heal Your Body* that 'Your brain is growing as you read these words', confirming how everything experienced causes microscopic changes in its cellular structure.

Imagine what that could mean. Every time you gaze at a picture of a crystal skull, something happens inside your own brain – some response is always provoked. Imagine the power of meditating with a real crystal skull! Current medical and psychological research shows just how quickly our brain can be entrained to change its patterns and responses. In just a short time new pathways are created within it that can demonstrate, for example, beneficial behaviour. As we shift our perceptions, we experience less stress and, with less stress, we can begin to heal our bodies, making them 'temples for the Spirit'.

Once again I was *remembering*. Once again crystal skulls and the human brain are connected.

Earthbound *Karma* and Our Ability to Change

Kalki's teachings indicate how *karma* (past action determining a person's present state) limits the human race. Doctors such as David Hamilton MD confirm that we can transform ourselves because the mind and body are intrinsically linked. Psychologists and philosophers point us towards the value of positive thinking.

Spiritual teachers throughout the ages have held the promise of enlightenment. Yet the 'wheel of karma' constantly turns. Something persistent seems to stop most of us from shifting beyond everyday perceptions and achieving our highest potential. *Karma* appears to lets us off the hook. Why?

Karma is an outdated attachment to Time, embedded deep in the fabric of our ancestral light body, and causing us to become locked into archaic control mechanisms. *Karma robs us of our true inheritance as beings of light having a physical experience.* Not only does it rob us in this life but in future lives too. Clearly we are not going to sit around and wait for our *karma* to be wiped out by the collapse of the magnetic field. There is something we can do now in a simple ceremony, when it is possible to release earthbound *karma* – once and for all. The requisite invocation only has to be said once and it is cleared (see Appendix 7).

Even if you choose not to clear your *karma* in this way, it is obvious we cannot all just carry on as previous generations did. Your mission, and mine, for which we incarnated, is not to disown our cosmic inheritance but to birth a newly-awakened consciousness. It includes planet-care and people-care, encompassing a wide environmental remit. This process, to change the dangerous directions that the human race has slid into, may occur in a split second of illumination or in the aeons of creative time between the occasion when a single cell grew in the slime of primeval Earth and our present day.

I became convinced that we need to make positive practical changes right now. You don't have to be wealthy, a political activist or a leader in society – simply an ordinary person whose heart is open to what original ancestral Maya wisdom teachers poetically called the 'Heart of the Earth', connecting our spiritual and our earthly roots. For us it is both an individual and collective attitude of mind, encompassing simplicity and respecting the place we hold as guardians of nature. Most importantly, when we are at peace with ourselves, we can express that peace to others, risking speaking from our hearts. These are the ways of empowerment, the ways of noble leadership and visionaries in any society.

I was reminded yet again of the power of the Mayan teachings at the 'Legend of the Thirteen Crystal Skulls' in New York in October 2010, an occasion when numerous famous crystal skulls were present. Four Mayan elders brought their messages and also spoke at a forum sponsored by the Society for Enlightenment and Transformation – the spiritual arm of the United Nations.

Kendall Ray Morgan, of Oracle Stone Productions, Arizona, co-organizer of this event, wrote the keynote speech presented by Grace Dale from Canada. It concluded:

> Perhaps this was why the ancient Maya, keepers of a calendar of unknown origin and surpassing technological complexity, chose to transmit a warning to us? Perhaps, as their great visionaries journeyed through the dimension of Time, they saw this defining moment that we call December 21st, 2012, and mapped it out for us in order to alert us to the doom that we alone – not the universe, not blessed Mother Earth – but that we alone have the power to bring down on our own heads.
>
> And perhaps it is not too late. For if the Maya were able to peer into the future, then they will have also seen that nothing is inevitable, that the power of choice remains with us – with each one of us as individuals, with each society, with each alliance of nations and ultimately with the whole of mankind. So although it cannot be doubted that we do indeed stand at a crossroads today, the Maya

also saw that we are not compelled to choose the road that leads to ruin and destruction.

But a new state of consciousness will have to be birthed amongst us if we are to avert disaster, if we are to take the right road, the good road that leads to a brighter tomorrow. This is entirely possible, not in the blink of an eye, not without hard work and dedication, but nonetheless it is still possible.

Do Re Mi

I recall a conversation with Mikhail, who said, 'Transforming our own consciousness can also change others' lives because of a resonant frequency that is set up inside the skull. When we embody a frequency of integrity and higher consciousness, it creates an intention which attracts the company of like-minded people. Resonance causes all of us to become part of the call to love and compassion, transcending limiting boundaries such as age, sex, race, creed, colour and time–space itself. Like an opera singer hitting a high piercing note, it becomes a beacon of empowerment as our aura is filled with light.'

For a fleeting moment, sadness descended upon me. I said, 'That beacon also announces our light to those who wish to oppose us for whatever reason, whether it be financial gain, karmic reasons or just ugly old-paradigm dominance. Sometimes all our skill is needed to hold our vision of Oneness, to embrace seemingly misguided ones for who they really are at core level. To show compassion to those most in need, or to those who appear less fortunate in their lives.'

Mikhail answered, 'You're right. No one said it would be easy. But once we have been filled with a higher light-frequency vibration there is no turning back.' Then he suddenly burst into song.

'Why are you singing?'

'I can't have you feeling sad about this. I was trying to cheer you up. As children, our early singing lessons were a reminder of our connections to the Moon, planets and Creation.' He sang it again, explaining as we went along.

Do: God in humanity

Re: *Regina Caeli*, Queen of Heaven, the Moon

Mi: Microcosmos, the Earth

Fa: Fatus, destiny, the planets

So: Sol, the Sun

La: *Voie Lacte*, the Milky Way

Si (*Ti*): Sidereal stars, galaxies, cosmos

Do: *Dominus*, God the Creator

Mikhail paused and smiled, saying, 'The *Mi* relates to an even older six-note scale called the *solfeggio*, that was suppressed by the early Roman Catholic Church. Would you believe, the frequency of *Mi* at 528 hertz was linked to transformation and miracles, even right down to changes at DNA level? It would be really neat to sing it to the crystal skulls.'

I commented, 'The fundamental notes of Creation are bringing us into harmony. We are singing out a new song, calling us to be generous with unconditional love and compassion, because it is not just our gift to give but a higher cadence that ultimately embraces all. In the language of the mystic, "We abide within the heart of God".'

I closed my eyes for a moment, thinking of emerging *Homo spiritus* as I slipped into a soothing blissful sleep.

·

CHAPTER TEN

Crystal Mysteries

Superconsciousness involves letting go of all that is immediate, tuning to the pulse of your life, breathing and listening to the beat of your heart, then rising through your energy field into the depths of your mind. Its forbidden secrets creep out of its dark corners, for the mind is expansive. Above and below – within you and beyond.

— FROM *THE MAYA END TIMES*, BY **PATRICIA MERCIER**

Flicking through a *National Geographic* over a cup of coffee, I came across a photo of giant selenite crystals found deep underground in northern Mexico. Seeing the vast size of the crystals compared to the geologists climbing over them, I wondered how many crystal temples are yet to be discovered deep within the Earth and what they might be like.

Then, glancing over to my desk, piled high with papers, I noticed my computer was on. It had powered up already. I was sure it had been off when I left. How could it have switched itself on overnight? Sweeping papers and books to one side, I saw a strange message across the screen. It was a series of numbers, repeating and repeating, going right across the screen:

12.19.19.17.19.12.19.19.17.19.12.19.19.17.19.12.19.19.17.19.

I sat looking at it in puzzlement. Glancing at my printer, it too suddenly started up and emitted a string of gobbledygook interspersed with heart signs, the word EVOLOVE, and a few astrological signs. I grabbed the printed page and stared at it.

I do have strange things happen to me, but this hadn't occurred before! Over the next few weeks I tried to juggle with the numbers, adding them up and assigning them all sorts of codes, but nothing made sense. I had never been good with numbers – probably something to do with using the right side of my brain for artistic and creative work. I was always too keen to find ways to expand my consciousness, and this had impinged on my more rational left brain.

Superstrings on the Threads of Time

Soozie had come to visit. She had no idea what the numbers could mean either. We sat with *Horus*, my time-travel crystal, between us, but just wishing *Shangri-La* our skull was here as well. She reminded me of the quotation about superconsciousness (page 148) and I responded, 'Yes, accessing superconsciousness is indeed possible – I am remembering so much, and now I am accessing the quantum field. My meditations, dreams, visions and hypnosis all confirm the existence of other dimensional states of being, assisting in the evolution of humanity.'

'Lucky you, doing all that deep work with *Shangri-La* before she was stolen!' she said. 'But others in my circle of friends would think I was crazy if I talked like you do about energies and dimensions.'

I went on to explain something she could say to her doubting friends. 'Just think calmly for a minute, this isn't so crazy. For instance, look at the ten different dimensions that quite rational superstring theorists in mainstream science are proposing. I've got them written down somewhere – ah, here they are. These ten dimensions are: length, breadth, depth, duration or time, probable future, a line from the Big Bang to infinity, infinity and all possible timelines, different infinities, folding the different infinities in upon themselves, and all possible timelines and all possible universes.'

'What an idea! But I'll have to be selective,' exclaimed Soozie. 'It sounds cool. Can't wait to try it out on them.' Then she kept pressuring me to tell her all about my hypnosis with Alice.

How the Crystal Skulls Were Born

I told Soozie about my past-life hypnosis experience, asking her to bear in mind the ten dimensions and how many theories have become factual realities as scientific reasoning catches up with the bow wave of human advancement.

Alice, the regressionist, had suggested, 'Leave your body and, flying up and up, see it below you. You are free, expansive, being drawn to a particular time and place. It is drawing you to it. Descend into another body, time and place.'

After a silence, I spoke. 'I see a lot of light. There's a large cave, a strange light and I can see the planets streaming past. Yes, it's light. A flat disc of stone is in front of me like a table, but not a table. It has a kind of power, like a wheel but not a wheel. There is a square hole in the middle. Grooves cut into the stone are glowing with blue light, so there is power coming from it. Little tiny people are sitting around the stone disc …'

Alice asked, 'Tell me about these little people.'

I whispered that I could only see their heads and shoulders, not their bodies. However, I was quite tall and thin with a slender face, completely different to normal, and my arms and legs were long, like those on an extraterrestrial body. I was looking down at the little people around the stone.

'They are chattering or singing or chanting, focusing on the disc and the light. They are there in the cave for the particular purpose of materializing a crystal skull. They tell me the skull has to be assembled by light, made of light. That's the way the information comes.

'It's put together in the light into its shape, and the square hole holds it until it's fully arrived and formed. It's a crystal skull, a really big one, shining. I don't know what the little people are actually doing, but I guess they need to be there. It's forming into shape in front of me.

'The lines of blue light on the stone are holding the energy coming through. I don't know how it is coming, except that there is light everywhere and the stone focuses it. It's becoming more and more beautiful and shining, and this large crystal skull of quartz is being moulded by the light. It's hot in places, it's red, very hot as it forms. It's coming from a long, long way to be here … There's something I can't quite catch … Oh yes, the little people are going to take it to Earth.'

Alice asked: 'So you are not on the Earth? Where are you?'

I tell her I don't know, and the little people aren't Earth people. I repeat that they are going to take the newly-born crystal skull to Earth.

Alice suggests to me: 'Now you are taking this skull to Earth with the little people ...'

'Yes, I'm in a beautiful jungle. There's a city with towers and pyramids, but it's not the Maya architecture I know, it is lighter. Like it's in a different dimension, with the little people and the crystal skull, and they are carrying it and taking it to this city. They place it in the centre of a very bright room. People are around the crystal skull now, looking, not doing anything.

'I am tall still, and I am watching. I know that the purpose of the skull is to be a keeper of energies and focus ... it's what the Earth needs.' I realize it is a wisdom-keeper crystal skull, one of many that once were placed at key points on the Earth.

I emphasized, *Earth needs this skull to help it keep focused and to keep light coming in*. That's what the crystal skull is going to do. The little people will look after it in that Earth dimension.'

I told Alice, 'I am withdrawing, taking my energy away. I have done what I needed to do, just witnessing, just seeing ...'

The Story of the Thirteen Crystal Skulls

When Soozie next visited, I explained the connection between the thirteen crystal skulls and the Nine Lords of Time, who are destined to 'descend'. I then delved deeper into stories originating from indigenous ancestral knowledge, about the reappearance of thirteen original singing skulls which will be placed in a specific energy alignment.

With great conviction I said to her, 'When the time is right for the chosen thirteen to manifest in this dimension, they will bring an age of peace to the world.'

During my quest I had become convinced that crystal skulls are calling out to souls who worked with them in other lifetimes.

Light codes in our DNA carry this 'memory', and this is how we are prompted into remembering information coming from other times or dimensions. Hence my hypnosis experience of the 'birth' of a crystal skull shows my own previous connections with them.

Another example of the appearance of the skulls comes from Bill Homan, guardian of the Mitchell-Hedges Skull of Love. He regards it as the original skull, from which a group of twelve were copied. Maya wisdom teachers shed more light on this, saying it was the gods who copied it, around 3,600 years ago.

Joanne van Wijgerden, the crystal skull guardian, has a number of different skulls. She has a Star Being or ET skull (carved from a kind of crystal called Larimar), a rose quartz normal skull and a half human-size black obsidian skull named *Orisa*. She revealed another facet of the crystal puzzle. She had focused on the civilization of Lemuria, where apparently there was no need for crystal skulls because the kind of humans alive at that time were completely at one with all that is.

I put my question to Joanne: 'What was the role of crystal skulls in the past, and what is their role today?'

It was only during Atlantean times, or right before that, that the crystal skulls appeared. They were there as wisdom keepers. Legends talk about twelve human-size crystal skulls that were carved as the main wisdom keepers, with a thirteenth skull that manifested from higher dimensions.

As human beings increasingly violated the cosmic law, the twelve skulls disappeared – they were scattered around the world – and the thirteenth skull was de-manifested again.

Nowadays the skulls are reappearing to help us connect to this cosmic information, which is also part of the Earth

– though we call it cosmic. In each skull a different being manifests, with a different role, which develops in contact with its keeper.

I made a strong connection with Joanne's words about a different being that is associated with each skull. Bill Homan made another important link, saying that his crystal skull is a life-form, an entity. It caused me to recall the Nine Lords of Time, bearing the skulls through the dimensions of Time.

Another aspect of the intrigue about the thirteen crystal skulls concerned twelve sacred planets orbiting different suns – the 'grandmothers' where human life was once found millennia ago, recounted at length in *The Mystery of the Crystal Skulls* by Chris Morton and Ceri L Thomas. The original skulls coming from these planets had a separate moveable jaw and were termed 'singing skulls', while others made later, perhaps 52 in total, were called 'talking skulls'. If asked, these skulls would respond appropriately regarding their origins and where they came from. Many skulls also have the ability to communicate back to Source and, as Joanne said, to dematerialize.

I am convinced that the singing skulls were the sole reason for building the huge Pyramid of the Sun at Teotihuacán, Mexico, above the secret Cave of the Skulls. Whilst writing *The Maya End Times* a few years ago, I began to question people I met about this cave. Was this cave a secret place of the skulls? Did all thirteen skulls manifest into earthly existence there, sent from other life forms in the galaxy, as the myths relate? Is it possible that the thirteen skulls alternate between being visible and invisible, and is that why people on Earth keep searching for all of them but can't find them?

What better indication could there be of the importance of the city? It was revered as a place where divine beings once trod, where the thirteen skulls were manifested and kept within an Ark. Bringing the whole story together, while these thirteen could have come from the 'grandmother' planets, they are now manifesting on Earth due to the influence of the Lords of Time. In some enigmatic way the Lords of Time know that the thirteen skulls embody the wisdom needed to take us beyond our four familiar dimensions, into a new paradigm and the birth of the spiritual human.

Star Johnsen-Moser gave another slant to this mystery by telling me about thirteen ancient Himalayan crystal skulls she had worked with. I had asked her what the connection was, if any, between the ancient Central American and Himalayan crystal skulls. Her reply, and evidence of another set of thirteen skulls under the guardianship of a different race, was as follows:

I have had the experience of doing intensive spiritual work with two ancient Central American crystal skulls and thirteen old or ancient Himalayan skulls. I am very much honoured to be the new caretaker of *Amakua*, an ancient bluish-coloured quartz crystal skull, thought by some to be 10,000 years old, which was discovered in a cave in the Himalayas. It is one of the original thirteen Himalayan crystal skulls acquired in 2002 by Dr Frank Loo from Hong Kong.

From the very first time I connected with these skulls, I had an inner knowing that they were Tibetan and had been used by Tibetan lamas for many generations. I felt that they had probably been hidden in caves along with other artefacts that were found with them (including Dropa discs), to keep them safe from the invading Communist Chinese.

The energy of these skulls was really very amazing and

cosmic, and we did some wonderful activation ceremonies and light-body activations in various locations in the USA. However, when a very huge and powerful high Lama presence came to me and allowed me to feel the pain of the Tibetan people for all that they have lost, I had to walk away from the skulls.

In conclusion I can say that, in my work with the Mayan skull *Max* and the Tibetan skull *Amakua*, the connections have ended up taking me to the same place.

The Enigma of Time and Light Codes

Once again my thoughts became focused on the enigma of Time in connection with the thirteen skulls. During 2008, when Lion-fire, shaman and crystal skull guardian, was visiting Britain, I meditated with his red jadeite Himalayan skull. The idea began to dawn that, at one time, there were four centres of spiritual focus in the world where sets of thirteen crystal skulls had appeared. This makes 52 skulls. As it happens, 52 is a key number in the Maya count of Time, connected with both the *T'zolk'in* calendar and the Pleiades stars.

Let me explain. There are rumours of a hidden group of skulls from Lemuria and Atlantis – both dematerialized from the Earth realms. Added to the thirteen skulls from Asia and the Americas, this makes four centres. My insights were deepened by Maya elders telling me that the magnetic centre of spiritual initiation once shifted from the Himalayas to Central America. When this occurred, the third group in physical existence, the Himalayan crystal skulls, would have been carefully hidden in remote caves or monasteries awaiting a future emergence.

The fourth group of thirteen skulls, ready to carry a new

spiritual impetus, manifested in the lands later known as southern USA, Mexico, Guatemala and Honduras. How long ago this spiritual shift occurred, only Great Spirit knows. But people who have worked with the ancient skull *Max*, whose history bridges East and West, say he is around 36,000 years old.

A few really ancient skulls hold a very special presence, a clarity and intent of purpose not found in younger skulls. They are record-keepers of Earth's history and, perhaps, carry guidance which has been encoded from the guardian beings of Earth and the other eleven planets. These skulls embody a sacred language of light containing words of power and encoded keys that some of their keepers channel.

Kathleen Murray in Scotland is a very accomplished healer and the guardian of a number of unusual skulls I have been fortunate to encounter. Her insights explain light codes and the opening of dimensional doorways within our brains. This is how Kathleen describes her skulls:

Mahasamatman or *Sammie* is quartz, of extraterrestrial origin, manifesting from light from Orion. He holds the records of Orion, similar to Earth's Akashic records. As to his age, he is eternal.

Kalif is a contemporary Brazilian smoky quartz, enhydro and with elestial crystals growing inside, carved in China.

Jade is carved in nephrite jade and was found in a temple in Mongolia. Her age is unknown. Academic sources date her up to 10,000 years, but she could be as much as 128,000 years old – dependant on concepts of the age of evolved civilizations of humanity.

The Twins are a double ancient skull ('two-faced'), weighing less than a kilo. They are carved of nephrite jade and were also found in a temple in Mongolia – age unknown.

Upon meditating with this powerful group of skulls, Kathleen told me more. 'They send out codes which awaken the "spiritual brain" we all have.' This is interesting, I thought, having regard to the 'sacred pyramid' within our own skulls.

'They use vibrational calls in a yet inaudible range to the human ear, but as near as they can to match the visual range of more evolved human beings. What I take this to mean is that it is possible sometimes for humans to see the light codes transmitted by the skulls, but not to hear them yet. I think the suggestion is that, in the activation of our spiritual brains, seeing can come before the hearing evolves. I find it does make sense scientifically.'

The pyramid of awareness in my head, my 'spiritual brain', affirmed that accessing the light codes of these skulls permits positive choices upon future Threads of Time. The core essence of my quest, to look to the future and the destiny of our fragile Earth, was confirmed. I knew that humanity has some hard choices to make. My quest further revealed that twelve ancient crystal skulls will manifest together when humanity has evolved. Only then will the thirteenth lock into place, to complete the sacred circle.

The real heart of this matter is placed before us when we take responsibility for our own actions, from our own hearts, reaching into our 'spiritual brain'. At that point, waking up to our destiny, we will fully understand why our present industrial-technological age hasn't been the right time for all of the skulls to be together again. We must first engender peace within and around ourselves.

As we have seen, and as Kathleen confirms with her comment about activation of our spiritual brains, we are poised for rebirth through superconsciousness – since we are in the ninth time of birthing the spiritual age of man in Aquarius. Simultaneously, we are entering Year Zero in the Maya count of Time, which begins the Fifth Creation, in 2012. At this auspicious time we can delay no longer in taking every opportunity presented to us to evolve into *Homo spiritus*.

The Lords of Time Speak

Meditation is key to this evolution. Every full moon, Mikhail and I, as Maya Solar Initiates, take part in worldwide group meditations, the initiative of Mayan elders. They are quite unrelated to the Skullmeet meditations on my blog site.

On one occasion, we had no other human companions with us, so we placed *Shangri-La* in our circle in the east direction of the rising Sun, Horus with the ancestors in the west. Mikhail stood in the north and I in the south. Our focus, and that of all the other groups meditating at this time, was the ancient Maya sacred city of Calukmul, and the day was 5 *B'atz'* (5 *Chuen* in Yucatec), regarded as a positive day for evolution.

Mikhail began by blowing a large Mexican conch shell trumpet. It is an intense sound to call other-dimensional beings into ceremony. At the same time it activates the sacred pyramid in one's skull. The sound was ringing in my head, like bells announcing the arrival of spirit guardians from Calukmul. This was going to be a wild journey! My inner senses were buzzing – there was none of the usual calm associated with meditation.

In my mind's eye I was whisked off. Suddenly, dense lush rainforest was all around, overgrowing a huge crumbling pyramid right in front of me. My senses filled with light as a beam of illumination came down from above, piercing the pyramid, as though it was splitting in two, revealing the inner core construction of a perfect temple.

Then, seemingly in some holographic projection plucked out of the Akashic Record, I saw a full moon ritual taking place. People were moving in and out of my visual range, fading into the trees, merging with the stones. Holding the central focus was a shining crystal skull, set upon a jaguar-shaped altar. I was 'told' it was Itzamná's Crystal Skull of the Night, the very one he brought to Earth in the time before Time began.

This picture wasn't to last. I moved rapidly through other dimensions. Words and colours sped through the innerscape of my mind. Suddenly the image of the Moon ritual vanished, and I returned to find myself once again in our sacred space. I had briefly witnessed something from the past. Was this to do with the combination of *Shangri-La* and my time-travel crystal? Or was it the conch trumpet that woke up an old memory?

I related to Mikhail what had occurred. He was insistent, 'Was there anything else you remember?'

'Yes, words, many words, and I could understand some of them, but not all. They were saying … *we descend from the past to tell you of your future … thirteen skulls of light, guiding the world … speaking mind to mind, speaking in tongues.* An assembly of enlightened beings. A huge screen, like a television … messages … our minds asking, the skulls answering … responses forming on the screen. The prophetic words: *we are the ones we have been waiting for …*'.

I paused, lost in the memory.

'Mikhail, the Lords of Time were speaking in my head. In some way they are reincarnating into this planetary vibration, this level or dimension, through the medium of the crystal skulls. It is the way they can best show us how to relate our hearts to our heads. They are assisting the peaceful growth of humanity, guiding those who are choosing love over fear, helping those who want to leave a viable Earth environment as a garden for their children and grandchildren, seven generations into the future – just as so many indigenous ancestral peoples have related to us.'

Mikhail suggested something quite outrageous: 'I think that, as well as seeing into the past, you picked up a future Thread of Time. You may well have heard a warning message from the thirteen skulls. What happens if technology runs out of control before a critical mass of people wake up? What will the future of humanity hold then? I suggest that, in that technologically advanced age, there will be a direct interface between computers, crystal energies and our minds. So one would only have to mentally ask a question of the skulls through the screen you mentioned, and they would give the answer. They might even use holographic projections to illustrate a point'.

'If that's true, then you mean the human race is heading toward a future when computers will become the physical manifestation of the Akashic Record – of all that ever was and ever will be?'

'Yes, I do! The Akashic Record will be downloaded to a very advanced physical computer system.'

'No, it couldn't really happen like that', I insisted. 'The Akashic Record is locked into fields of consciousness surrounding the Earth and connecting to the whole interdimensional Creation Field. It is melded into the mind of *Hunab K'u*, the Maya One Giver of Movement and Measure and space–time. I don't think the crystal skulls would ever 'give' their power to computers, even highly-advanced, spiritually-evolved ones. They will always want to link directly to sensitive people who value wisdom.'

'Okay, I agree with you. Just testing! I wanted to see how far I could push your imagination!'

Then he quoted some words from the 1960s new consciousness movement. 'Here's to the crazy ones. The misfits. The rebels. The troublemakers. The round pegs in the square holes. The ones who see things differently. They're not fond of rules, and they have no respect for the *status quo*. You can quote them, disagree with them, glorify or vilify them. About the only thing you can't do is ignore them. Because they change things. They push the human race forward. While some may see them as the crazy ones, we see genius. Because the people who are crazy enough to think they can change the world are the ones who do.'

In the moonlight I could see a wide, mischievous smile spreading across Mikhail's face.

·

CHAPTER ELEVEN

Maya Cosmovision
and the Never-Ending Dream

Namaste is an ancient Sanskrit blessing, meaning, 'I honour the place within you where the entire universe resides. I honour the place within you of love, light, truth and peace. I honour the place within you where, when you are in that place in you and I am in that place in me, there is only one of us.'

– RAM DASS

My journey of exploration was finally revealing how chang- ing human consciousness highlights the relevance of crystal skulls in the enigma of Time. I continued with my quest through hypnosis, learning how to tune the crystal skull in my head to consistently take me into superconsciousness, when necessary.

By contrast I received worrying information about time travel and technology accessing the quantum field, from a source I had begun to have serious doubts about. I include it here because I feel that all facets of my crystal skull experiences are as valid as my traditional initiations. It did, however, cause me to change the names of the two friends involved in this process, for their and my own peace of mind.

The Gift of the Skull

There was more to my past life hypnosis session. I told Alice, 'Everything is black. No body. No images, no mind. I am resting.' So she asked me, 'Shall we go on or come back?'

I whispered that I would go on, because the blackness was clearing. Then I slipped into to being Eloha, a young Indian woman, another part of myself whom I had encountered in a previous session. I (or Eloha) was standing on high rocks over-looking a canyon, having climbed there because I had to take my father's prayers and offer them on the day of a solar eclipse.

I said, 'I understand what's happening on an eclipse. The dark-ness doesn't frighten me because I go into the darkness and find the light. I do that for the people. I take their prayers and find the light, step into the light …

'I can travel in the light. I travelled to a time when the crystal skull was being born, but there is more to remember …'

Alice asked me, 'Where are you now Eloha?' I replied, 'Still above that rocky canyon and seeing the Sun going down. My feet are stamping out the fire, and I'm collecting up a leather bag and starting to walk down a dusty path.'

In her soft voice, with the hint of a Canadian accent, Alice said, 'Go deeper. I am going to count to three. You will be in another significant part of that lifetime.' I then found I was in the same past life, but I experienced *two* of my selves, for I was Eloha and Alloa as well. (Alloa is my spiritual name, in my life today.)

By way of explanation, here is a quote from my book *The Maya End Times*:

Lifting up the heavy, tattered, old brown hide bag, pulled together with string, I was very curious, wondering what could possibly be within. I began to untie it. Just as I finished, a sudden cooling rush of wind spiralled down into the kiva from above. Looking up, through the birth hole, I sensed that the woman had gone, just disappeared, and I was left holding ... a crystal skull!

A *kiva* is a subterranean room in the American southwest, used for rituals by the ancient Pueblo peoples.

'I am in the kiva. I pick up the bag and in it is the crystal skull that the old woman gave me in the kiva in my book!' (Laughing) 'I am holding it. But also at the same time I'm the woman Eloha, and when I am old I am going to give the skull to Alloa in the kiva because it's a dreaming place.'

Alice asked, 'What's happening?'

'I am connecting. Remembering that Alloa is Patricia's spiritual name. I am the old woman now, giving the crystal skull to Alloa.' I paused for a long while as I tried to work out something very strange. 'I am the old lady Eloha who climbed down the ladder, and I am Alloa as well! I have the tatty leather bag tied up with string, sitting there between us. Alloa is sitting in the kiva. The old lady is sitting there too.'

Alice asked: 'Are you the old lady? Are you going now?'

'Yes. I am climbing up the ladder. It's very hard – my bones are stiff and it's difficult to climb. Then I start walking through the desert and I walk a long, long way. It is my last walk, because I have given the crystal skull to Alloa.'

Alice was moving me on: 'I want you to go to the point where you are leaving that body. Tell me about it.'

'I am just curled up … warm … I am travelling. It's a dark, dark river. The water is taking me on. I know that it takes me on to the light, travelling until the water becomes liquid light, and then I will be reborn. But not yet.'

'Do you want to go further or stay in that peace?'

'I would like to come back now.'

That was the end of my hypnosis sessions. They had opened up interesting dreamtime paths, giving me another explanation of sorts for my fascination with crystal skulls in this lifetime. But I needed to make sense of everything that was happening to me, for when I thought about it more, the experience with the crystal skull in the hypnosis was very strange indeed. It's not every day that you find two lives converging – and they are both yours!

My hypnosis sessions into the past and future opened up parallel timelines. I shouldn't really have been surprised, but I was. I thought deeply about it for some weeks, absorbing the experiences at soul level.

Time Travel

My strange experiences backwards and forwards in Time, both during hypnosis as well as with crystal skulls, were nothing compared to the information Soozie's friend Karl sent me concerning the secret time travel program of DARPA (the US Defense Advanced Research Projects Agency) that occurred in the 1970s. He told me of experiments where actual teleportation and time travel apparently occurred – when a person moves physically from one time–space to another.

During one experiment conducted for the purpose of evaluating time travel in 1972, a young person found himself in a scenario in year 1863. Researchers apparently found an old photograph of him. He said in an interview, 'I ended up becoming the first time traveller from the future to be photographed!'

Karl was obsessed with what he called a truth campaign exposed by exopolitics and these ideas of DARPA achieving teleportation time travel into past and future events. He kept telling me that Tesla-type equipment as well as futuristic electro-optical methods like the chronovisor were used to access the quantum field.

This information really spooked me for a while. It led me to think that Karl's and Mikhail's warnings about my use of the internet might have a basis in reality. The prospect that a way of accessing the quantum field had been reached some forty years earlier left me wondering how much further has this been explored. I realized that crystal skulls could be put to unscrupulous use if a technological way was found to 'read' the information they hold.

It certainly didn't seem the right use for them. I was very uncomfortable with this idea – there were military and control implications. Much better that the skulls stay in the safekeeping of their guardians, to be activated only when giving information in a telepathic way by scrying, meditation or shamanistic insights. I felt I needed to be on my guard. Just as well, as things turned out.

I was enjoying the English springtime when I received a message from Karl. 'It's a grim picture. We need to meet. Leave your mobile phones behind and go to the phone box outside Starbucks. I'll call you there.'

When we did so, Karl said, 'Meet you in the park by the river in 20 minutes. Make sure you are not followed.'

Mikhail and I, both curious, went to meet him. Looking pale and severe, he said, 'Let's talk as we walk along the riverbank. No security cameras here. Listen, I haven't even told Soozie about this, but I think you and Mikhail are in danger.'

'What? Please explain. And why no mobile phones?'

'So *they* can't track you, of course.'

'Oh, Karl, isn't this a bit over the top?' exclaimed Mikhail.

'Look, friends, I'm serious. Patricia, you should know just how easy it is to put someone under hypnosis. Just imagine what could be done with mind-altering drugs! But, anyway, what I'm talking about is different, very different, and it's about using the quantum field to access people's minds.'

Mikhail urged me, 'Tell Karl what's been happening with the meditations organized through your blog site.'

'Well, a particular day and time is chosen, and everyone meditates at the same time. It's simple. We are given some images to focus upon.'

'What if there are images given to you that you don't see with your eyes, but your brain takes on, just like subliminal advertising before it was supposedly banned on TV in the 1970s? There could be mind-control going on, and you don't even realize it.'

I looked aghast and Mikhail continued, 'She even gets a phone message sent to remind her when to meditate.'

Karl said, 'So what if there are also subliminal sounds being sent to everyone who is meditating? Certain low frequencies could be beamed to you that are very damaging, and you wouldn't consciously hear them as audible sounds because they're below normal hearing range.' Remembering how astronauts got sick when their bodies no longer received the vibrational frequency of planet Earth, I realized how powerful infra-sounds can be.

'At the very least, these people could be using the mobile phone to track you. You know the way they do it: when you arrive in another country, your phone registers that by switching net-works,' went on Karl.

'What do you mean, *these people?*'

'A clandestine World Order', continued Karl. 'They could be selecting and using sensitive people, just like you, who are all meditating together, and grooming them for future memory experiments. Maybe they are "conditioning" you because of your ability to shift dimensions using that old crystal skull of yours.'

Walking along the peaceful river on this sunny afternoon, this didn't seem likely, but Karl was insistent. 'Some of these dimensions have been hacked into, and negative energy has been implanted there. That's why so many people have bad experiences in other-dimensional realities. All that was set up a long time ago. Now the World Order is surfing what you call the Threads of Time, selecting and converging them into their desired manipulated image of the future.'

Mikhail and I stopped and looked at each other. 'That couldn't really happen ... or could it?'

'I could tell you about an experiment right out of the pages of science fiction. Just shut up and listen,' urged Karl rudely. 'All the "sensitives" are disappearing. Only one person, or one "thing", knows where. But every indication suggests they are being herded into paradise gardens with glass-caged biodome covers from which they can't escape. Each one is permanently sealed to prevent the quantum field of light and life penetrating. From inside they can see the biodome around them – they are still going about "normal" lives.

'But their psychic abilities are being modulated, monitored and manipulated, then regularly extracted from the sealed zone. Then these entrained psychic abilities are used to control the remaining global population in a hypnotic way, to keep them "asleep", just as the old Maya gods "blinded" humanity.

Freethinkers are particularly targeted because their energy is rarefied, of high frequency, and it's this energy that the experimenters use to control Time for their own ends.'

'What would happen to those poor people?' I gasped.

'In such an experiment, at first they wouldn't know where they were. But then they would see the paradise garden and be fooled into thinking they were in a safety-bubble. As the extremes of capitalism have become even more extreme, "negative freedom" has been developed as a psychological control mechanism. People would be told they were in the biodome to protect them from pandemic diseases or nuclear radiation, although actually all of that would be an illusion. Eventually though, disconnected from the quantum life-field, the sensitives' bodies would decay, leaving only a madness in their brains which would not die because they'd been insulated from natural time in the biodome.'

'Look Karl,' I said. 'We don't believe you. We've always deliberately avoided getting drawn into this cultural fear-based way of living, sucking into one conspiracy theory after another. We don't scare that easily, and we are both going to carry on as normal.'

Karl kept glancing nervously back over his shoulder. Beneath his dark skin he looked pale and drawn. I had never seen him like this before. His last remarks were, 'Patricia, at the very least, agree with me that crystal skulls need protection, because they are showing us some hidden laws of the universe and they are part of vast meditation networks. There could be manipulators around that would stop at nothing to prevent the evolution of human consciousness.'

We parted company. 'Did you actually believe any of that way-out stuff?' I asked Mikhail later.

'I'm not sure. But as a precaution, you should be careful and stop all your internet meditations for a while. Let's go back to our mountain retreat in Spain and live very simply, just meditating with the crystals you have, with the pine trees and the energies of the land.'

Still feeling dismissive of Karl's warning, and pretending I wasn't shaken by this episode, I nevertheless changed my blog habits and closed down the Skullmeet site. We just disappeared off the radar for a while.

Grandmother Keeper of the Skulls

I generally avoid immersing myself in negative thinking, dubious intrigue and conspiracy theories. I can see all too easily how one's outlook on life can become fear-ridden. Nevertheless, I err on the side of caution when it comes to more serious things. It's a bit like the old superstition of saying 'touch wood' for protection.

I prefer to keep my mind uncluttered – this has been crucial to developing the golden crystal skull energy within. I find I can access some profoundly deep truths of shamanism that cross dimensional boundaries. Whenever I am able, I go to see a Yucatec calendar shaman I know, who lives in the remote, dry scrubland of Quintana Roo, Mexico. I seek him out in his humble abode, a palm-thatched wooden building called a *palapa*. It's simple but effective – waterproof in the heavy rains, withstanding hurricanes and providing shade. Chan and his family of four sleep in hammocks in the only room in the *palapa*, and they cook in a small lean-to shed.

I listen attentively to Chan because I am fascinated by predictions and the dire prophecies of the Chilam Balaam 'Jaguar Prophet', written in the form of poems, some say around the end of the 15th century. These prophecies seem to have foreseen what is happening in the world today with disease and war, not to mention natural disasters on a huge scale.

Maya teachers have explained to me that we can ameliorate dramatic Earth changes and our impact upon the Earth by illuminating our consciousness, living lightly and ethically. They stress that our consciousness, called *Ol* in the Itzá Maya language, is the one thing that will make a difference since we are all part of the whole, from the smallest atom to the most distant galaxy. When the Maya speak of *Ol*, it is not just our everyday consciousness, or for that matter our *un*consciousness, that occurs during anaesthesia or heightened semiconscious states of mind such as daydreaming, hypnosis or imagining. They mean an encompassing superconsciousness embracing all this and cosmic consciousness too – their cosmovision.

I described it in *The Maya End Times* after gazing into the starry depths of my crystal skull. 'Superconsciousness is the determination of full awareness, of being fully present. It is the faculty by which one knows one's own existence.' And again, 'Some of you say that consciousness may exist after death or before birth. But that is inaccurate. It is through superconsciousness that we understand that each of us has an everlasting flame or divine light within. With superconsciousness we know that there is existence in those other realms of which your shamans speak, including after-death and before-birth. Like the little facets of a crystal, we are always linked and we are always part of the whole.'

Mikhail and I value these clear links in the metaphysical worlds and the realm of superconsciousness. We have always wished to keep our channels and connections to the quantum field, the web of life and light, open. Chemicals and drugs, even medically prescribed ones, could change that for us. We never deliberately seek out mind-altering drugs or plant substances – they are appropriate only in traditional ceremony or initiation overseen by a skilled shaman.

So we had complete trust in Chan when he invited us to stay

overnight in his lush garden for a vision quest seeking the nature spirits. I also had a premonition it could be a way to reconnect with my crystal skull *Shangri-La*, wherever she was. I realized much later that the day we had decided to go to Chan's was 8 *Tijax* (8 *Etznab*), the obsidian-blade day that heralds the power of cutting, solving, bringing mysteries to light.

Around a week later we were sitting in Chan's garden, which was full of fruiting trees of every juicy variety, watching a motley family of chickens scratching in the dirt beneath them. Violet bougainvillea cascaded wildly around the jagged perimeter fence of spiny nopal cactus. Mikhail and I settled down on an old woven blanket and Chan passed us a gourd cup filled with a dark, strong smelling brew.

'It's *balché*,' he said, nodding encouragingly at us.

This is going to be powerful, I thought. *Balché* is made from fermented tree juices, honey and herbs, and it is the local hallucinogenic drink. Although we had tasted small sips of it before in ceremonies, this was clearly going to be different, as we were asked to drink cup after cup.

I knew that, by drinking it, my perceptions would change. I placed my ceremonial necklace and *Horus* the time-travel crystal on a stone altar amongst the vegetation. I lit candles and scattered an offering of copal incense on the small fire Chan had started.

Mikhail said to me, 'Remember that *balché* shifts your normal dimensions, because of particular plant vibrations you are ingesting.'

'Yes, I know. The ancient shaman-kings used a variety of herbs when seeking visions. Perhaps *balché* will open a gateway to superconsciousness – what Chan calls *Ol*. Maybe then I will be able to go deeper with the golden crystal skull within my head. Perhaps I can reach for a strand of Time Future and discover exactly how human consciousness will evolve.'

Having experienced meditation and hypnosis, I now needed to delve deeper into other realities, to return with new knowledge to where I started. I had to know how to get back!

Chan arranged his *sastoon* stones around the fire and I placed my travelling crystal there too. I said to myself that it may be small but size is unimportant, because it has been activated in the company of many crystal skulls during ceremonies and meditations. Glancing across at this crystal by the fire, I could sense my ordinary consciousness was already changing. Mikhail and I agreed that we would keep talking to each other for as long as possible, in order to have a better chance of cross-referencing what happened.

I relaxed and let go of my day-to-day inconsequential thoughts as I slipped into a heightened state. I began to see a fine thread of silver light, like an umbilical cord stretching from the sacred pyramid in my head and reaching upwards into the branches of the tree above me. Looking around, I could see other threads, just like mine, reaching up from Mikhail and Chan into the same tree. I began to understand these were our connections with the mythic Tree of Life. We were the living fruits, each and every one of us on fruiting branches of an enormous World Tree.

The physical space between my crystal and the fire was changing, becoming misty. I couldn't see the altar under the trees at all, but I could smell the sweet copal. My familiar world was dissolving. The fire was livening up, crackling and sparking, sending little messages up to the stars. I heard Mikhail saying, 'Remember to come back the way you go in, Patricia – it's vital!'

'Mikhail,' I whispered, taking another sip of *balché*, 'There's a lake right there, between me and the altar over there, that's getting bigger. Volcanoes are erupting. The Earth is very young. Rainbows, there are rainbows everywhere. The rainbows are giving the land and the sky its colours. They are forming out of the mist, touching the surface of the lake. Wow, it's an enchanted place. It's Lake Atitlan, "the place where the rainbow gets its colours".'

The *balché* brew was taking effect. My words were sporadic.

'Pink, soft pink, then magenta. Clear sky blue, then deep ultramarine. Violet changing to heavy purple. Sparks of fire erupting from three volcanoes around the lake. It's dark, just a dark lake now. There are pink clouds above it. Strange shapes. Faces in them. Souls waiting to be born. More and more faces. I'm looking down into the lake, becoming a mirror and seeing a golden crystal skull hovering over it all. It's just hanging in the darkness, glowing, protecting. The water level of the lake is dropping, dropping ... people are appearing where there was once a lake.'

I pulled back from my vision. I got my mind to ask the question, 'How will human consciousness evolve?' But where was I? What dimension was I in? What time? I was confused.

Then I relaxed, allowing the *balché* plant spirits to take me to another level. I just *knew* I had to make the right choices, choose the right path.

Suddenly, everything was love. All was soft, but clear. I tried to keep talking, to describe it. 'Sublime love. Gentleness. Care. Compassion. It's everywhere, Mikhail. It's everywhere. Not just in this place. We can find love everywhere. We only have to open our hearts for it to come in ... the animals, birds, trees, insects, they all have it at their level of knowing ...'

I didn't want to leave that place. My heart was full. I heard Chan calling me, 'Señora, what do you see?' Mikhail's words came back to me: 'Remember to come back the way you went in.' I had to get back to the lake, but it wasn't easy. I just wanted to stay in the love. I saw the lake filling up again, people disappearing beneath the dark water.

Finally, I stood on the shores of Lake Atitlan, watching the pink clouds of souls lift up, watching the golden crystal skull get bigger, seeing it above my head, filling with gold crystalline light. Then in an instant I was back in Chan's magic garden. Somehow, my *Horus* crystal had moved from the altar to my side. Mikhail was stretched out asleep and Chan was pacing around, whisking a bunch of herbs through the air, putting more wood and incense on the fire.

Every so often he muttered words: '*Itzamná*, Dew of the Sky ... *Ixchel*, Divine Mother of Nature ... *Ku-kul-kaan*, Teacher of Love and Serpent of Wisdom ...'

These deities I knew, but every so often he would forcefully call upon others that were unknown to me: '*Ah-yum-kaak, Ix-yum-zuhuy-kaak*, god and goddess of fire ... *Ah-yum-ha, Ix-yum-ha*, god and goddess of water ... *Ah-yum-kaax, Ix-yumixmukane*, god and goddess of land and mountains ... *Ah-yum-ek, Ix-yum-ek*, god and goddess of stars ...'

The litany of gods and goddesses always concluded with '*Ix-Mukane*, wise and ancient grandmother, keeper of the skulls, come, be with us, guide us home.'

Our night with Chan ended. I felt something had shifted, but I wasn't sure if it was within me or in my experience of the world.

Waking up in Chan's garden to a bright morning, we set off again on our travels. The Day was 4 *Kej* (4 *Manik* in Yucatec) a highly positive sign concerned with the destiny of humanity and a vision of what is to come.

Driving through the hot, flat, state of Quintana Roo, we were pleased to reach the Gulf of Mexico where dry scrubland eventually gives way to lusher, thicker growth. It's a wild region peppered with *cenotes*, circular water holes measuring up to 40 metres across, formed in the limestone rock. They once provided the only available fresh drinking water for the ancient Maya. The stillness and depths of these *cenotes* was awesome. It reminded me of looking into the eyes of *Shangri-La*. There were other worlds hidden there. Oh, how I missed *Shangri-La*.

I took to 'speaking' to the goddess Ix-Mukane whenever I could, using Chan's words, 'Ix-Mukane, wise and ancient grandmother, keeper of the skulls, come, be with us, guide us home, guide us home, guide us home,' always adding, 'Please help me to find *Shangri-La* again.'

Perhaps it was Ix-Mukane herself who eventually provided the direction in which we had to go. We'd had no intention of retracing our journey and staying again in Guatemala City, but something was drawing us there. Perhaps Grandmother, keeper of the skulls, was calling us. Braving the traffic and negotiating narrow streets we searched for the hotel. Eventually we checked in at the same run-down little hotel with the same purple-painted receptionist.

Imagine our surprise as she handed me my day-pack. It was complete with the crystal skull!

We had left it behind – it hadn't been stolen. 'I found it in the back of the wardrobe and kept it for you.' She said this with that characteristic honesty and broad, open smile typical of so many of the Maya people we've met.

.

CHAPTER TWELVE

Quantum Time

Human consciousness is not a permanent fixture: cultural anthropology testifies that it developed gradually in the course of millennia. In the 30,000 or 50,000 year history of modern human beings, the human body did not change significantly, but human consciousness did. How will it change next? The answer to this question is of more than theoretical interest: it could decide the survival of our species.

– FROM *QUANTUM SHIFT IN THE GLOBAL BRAIN* BY **ERVIN LASZLO**,
AUTHOR, VISIONARY, NOBEL PEACE PRIZE NOMINEE

Shangri-La was back! The fears I had about malign influences affecting me through the internet had long since melted into the background. Thought after thought about the immense implications of the crystal skulls were dawning upon me. I realized that nothing less than morphogenesis and quantum evolution would produce a physical–spiritual evolution. Nurturing our individual spirituality is vital in this process so that human evolution can proceed beyond the Darwinian scientific barriers of modern life.

I continued to have deep dreams and visions. Times were difficult. Although I knew crystal skulls help us to maintain clear, open minds, obstacles have to be overcome, especially when we require new and positive directions to replace our increasingly unsustainable society.

Beacons of Light

Let me take you back a few years. Remember I had my 'time-keeper' quartz *Horus* with the crystal skull in Guatemala? Well, on this occasion I was sleeping with it under my pillow. I snuggled into the warmth of the bed. The bedside clock was ticking annoyingly. Mikhail stroked my head and calmed me. 'Try to get some rest – it's a big day tomorrow. It's your talk.'

Early morning light was filtering through the bedroom shutters. A cool breeze was blowing the voile curtain and night-time shadows on the wall turned into familiar surroundings as the light increased – plain white walls and a few wall-hangings and decorations we'd collected from our travels. I decided I should introduce the idea of the Platonic Year and the birth of the new humanity into the talk I was to give. It was entitled 'Crystal Skulls, the Quantum Universe and Healing'. I might even explain it using the idea of tortillas. The opening words kept sifting through my mind.

Today I am going to show links between quantum physics, crystal skulls and healing our bodies of light. To begin with, *quantum* is a Latin word that simply means 'how much'. It's nothing complicated. But it has been used to explain a very complex subject. When we look deeply into the science of quantum energy, it challenges many of our comfortable long-held beliefs. It challenges our concepts of 'smallest' and 'largest' It takes us into the quantum theory of 'entanglement', which Einstein joked was 'spooky action at a distance'.

Perhaps that's what happened to my computer and printer when the code numbers popped up, I thought, rather irrationally. I was irritated by it. I don't like unexplained happenings.

I tried to drop back to sleep for half an hour by stopping the inner chatter. But some of the words of my presentation kept going through my mind.

If I stand on a mountain and look at the distant stars, my mind reaches out towards them, covering astronomical distances in nanoseconds. Or if I look across at the sea 30 miles away, my mind stretches out just 30 miles. Either way, it's instantaneous and it's not just inside my brain that this experience is happening, but outside it too. Vision involves light impulses coming in to our eyes *and* an outward simultaneous projection of images. The idea is so simple yet hard to grasp. We all function in this way, and we do it automatically all the time. But since my experiences with crystal skulls, this and other fundamental aspects of life have become really clear to me.

I started getting sleepy, but still the words were going on and on.

I'm going to tell you about an experiment that took place at the University of Paris in 1982. A team of physicists discovered that, under certain circumstances, subatomic particles are able to communicate with each other. They can do this whether they are ten metres or ten billion miles apart. From this experiment eventually developed the concept of the Holographic Universe, and it made a mockery of Einstein's theory that nothing can travel faster than the speed of light. Since travelling faster than light is effectively breaking the time barrier, this really put the cat amongst the pigeons …

I was trying to find ways to juggle my words around, to make them more believable for sceptics who might be in the audience. Now I knew I wouldn't get back to sleep: like it or not, it would be midnight before I could rest again. The next morning I set off for my talk, feeling bothered.

I began speaking as planned, then continued:

You know what happened next? Big-name physicists and thinkers took up the problem, declaring variously that objective reality does not exist, that nothing is actually separate because separateness is an illusion, that the whole universe is an illusion, or that despite appearing to be solid, the universe is in essence a phantasm, a gigantic, intricate light-encoded hologram.

A hologram is a three-dimensional image, rather like a photograph, made with the aid of a laser. This image, captured on film, can be cut in half and then illuminated by another laser. Each half will contain the entire image and, moreover, if the halves are cut up repeatedly, each little bit will still contain the entire, but a smaller, image. So, unlike normal photographs, every part of a hologram contains a picture of the whole.

The interesting point I'm going to make is that of *natural* holograms. They are formed when human consciousness in wave form interacts with other wave forms creating interference patterns. Each of us leaves our holographic traces in the universal field, the web of light and life, the template of Creation. Imagine that! Generation after generation, nation after nation, leaving their ideas in a huge, encompassing hologram!

I paused to let my words take effect, 'And that is not all. Every living thing is also part of this web – even rocks and crystals.' I took a sip of water.

A good way to identify a particular crystal scientifically is to study its interference pattern, which is always specific to type. As a healer I use this knowledge because, if I place a crystal over a chakra area, the interference pattern of the crystal provides a stable pattern of perfection that is transmitted to the chakra through resonance. Additionally, if the right crystal is chosen, and if I'm channelling healing intentions, then the chakra and hence the person's body is beneficially affected.

Imagine what that means when we use a crystal skull for healing or meditation. It means that, at some level of our consciousness – our superconsciousness – we can access its energy fields. They hold unimaginable amounts of holographically-encoded information. Information held in a crystal skull can be transferred to another crystal or person through the medium of the web of light and life.

And this is not all. Crystal skulls are, according to their guardians, linking into a crystalline network or grid. It means their inherent power is exponentially increased by much more than the simple sum of the parts. In computer-speak, it means the skulls are the hardware through which software programming is taking place, involving humans. As this occurs, we shift through our crown chakra into the seventh-dimensional level and *theta* states of healing consciousness. We find the innerscape of Creation.

I thought my words were becoming rather heavy, so I turned to the slideshow, projecting stunning images of crystal skulls into the room. There were exclamations at the beauty revealed within them. People pointed and said, 'I can see a picture inside,' or 'That one is speaking in my head.'

So many souls were touched by the images that I asked them to focus upon the one that 'spoke' most loudly to them. I then suggested they visualize that crystal skull inside their own head. I proposed that they ask the crystal skull what it had to teach them, absorb that teaching, then to thank it and gently let the inner crystal skull fade from their mind.

Drawing them out of the meditation I projected my little mnemonic verse on the screen:

C crystals	S serenely
R remind	K knowing
Y you	U un-
S share	L limited
T talk	L light
A activate	S secrets
L love	

I noticed a number of people writing it down and was pleased that something so simple appealed to them. It was time to remind them that they didn't need their own crystal skull.

All the information you will ever need is inside your own skull. All the healing you will ever need is inside your own body.

The more you tell yourself that you really *are* a being of light, the more you will *remember* – yes, really *remember* – the plan of light and love that is working out on our beautiful blue-green planet. It was put into place aeons ago for just this moment, this precise time in human evolution. *We are ready to 'birth' a new consciousness.* Crystal skulls are beacons of light to show us the way.

And so my experiences with crystal skulls have shown me a different universe, even a number of multiverses. The classical philosophical view that 'All is One' has a firm basis in modern quantum science. It means that we are never separate, that light informs the very fabric of existence. Light at photon level, as a carrier of information, permeates every cell of our body, the land that is around us, the homes we dwell in – they are all influenced by light.

We are empowered beings of light. The ancient healing concepts of chakras – energy centres – are no longer regarded as separate 'wheels of light'. They are dynamic energy circuits within our bodies and an intrinsic part of the whole of Creation.

I flashed on-screen some inspirational words that can be used as an affirmation: *As visionaries, co-creators, we can paint the dream of a beautiful flowering Earth – it is up to each of us to make it happen.*

There are many ways we can paint that dream and unite with superconsciousness. We can listen to inspiring music, sing, dance, feel a deep connection to the beauty of nature. We can meditate or laugh with joy. Every time we enter *theta* consciousness, we transcend our ordinary selves. We enter another realm, a realm within the unlimited encompassing place of love. It is there that we find our deepest truth.

There is something beyond time, beyond space, beyond all the quantum laws of the universe that is calling us to these realms where a deep connection to Source abides. It is our choice to surrender to this call. Surrender means we shift to the path of a meaningful and purposeful life, releasing repetitive thought and behaviour patterns.

Along the way we take control of our health and our destiny. As each individual person shifts, a change takes place in collective consciousness. Eventually this evolves a critical mass of people into a new type of human – *Homo spiritus*.

I paused to let this take effect.

Crystal skulls show us images of clarity, reflections of perfection. The first key to access their light-encodements is to remember the adage 'As above, so below'. This is poetically written by Maya scribes as 'Heart of Heaven, heart of the Earth'.

The second key is to link this understanding to our hearts from the sacred pyramid of energy within our own skulls. It is only with our hearts that we can overcome the challenges modern life throws at us. Living in a heartfelt way is the only path open to us. We must make that choice. Not tomorrow or the next day, but *now*. Then, and only then, understanding becomes contemplation and contemplation becomes wisdom. This is simply put with the traditional verse:

Heart of Heaven, heart of the Earth,
Give us our sign, our word,
As long as there is day, as long as there is light.
When it comes to the sowing, the dawning,
Will it be a greening road, a greening path?
Give us a steady light, a level place,
A good light, a good place,
A good life and a beginning.

This was a positive point on which to end the talk, as I flashed my treasured collection of scenes from the natural world across the screen.

Solving a Mystery

Back home, Mikhail and I sat down for a well-deserved cup of tea. I talked to him again about the mysterious numbers that had appeared across my computer screen, together with the word EVOLOVE on the printer. The numbers

12.19.19.17.19.12.19.19.17.19.12.19.19.17.19.12.19.19.17.19.

had kept on repeating and repeating, right across the screen. I was still puzzled by it, but Mikhail had an idea. 'Those numbers look like a date to me.'

'Don't be silly, they're not a date, they're some sort of code.'

'Yes, they are both a date and a code.' Obviously he was going to take his time to reveal the answer to me. I was impatient. For weeks I had been thinking *what could this series of numbers be?*

Mikhail quoted some words he had read on a friend's website: '*When we change our attitude to Time, Time treats us differently.*

If we come better to understand our relationship with Time, we may better understand ourselves and others – wise young Dr Rock wrote that.'

Clearly Mikhail was setting up a mind-teaser for me. He wrote down the number sequence I'd seen, then some more figures underneath:

12.19.19.17.19.12.19.19.17.19.12.19.19.17.19.12.19.19.17.19.

13.0.0.0.0.13.0.0.0.0.13.0.0.0.0.13.0.0.0.0. 13.0.0.0.0. 13.0.0.0.0.

13.0.0.0.1.13.0.0.0.1.13.0.0.0.1.13.0.0.0.1.13.0.0.0.1.13.0.0.0.1.

'I'll give you a clue. Separate the lines of numbers into blocks of five. Then just write them like this:'

    12.19.19.17.19.

    13.0.0.0.0.

    13.0.0.0.1.

'I've got it!' I exclaimed. 'They're Maya Long Count dates!'

'Yes. Throughout history, dates were fixed by this calendar. The Long Count goes back thousands of years, but the current cycle began on a day equivalent to 11th August 3114 BCE, the start date of our present Fourth Creation.

'After December 21st, 2012 or, as the day-keepers say, Year Zero, we start a new count of Time, the Fifth Creation. In the Long Count the numbers increase one day at a time, but when written they don't go beyond 19 for the *katun*s, *tun*s and *kin*, or 17 for the *uinal*s.

'On the first line you've written down, there are 12 *baktun*s, 19 *katun*s, 19 *tun*s, 17 *uinal*s, 19 *kin*. On the second line, it's 13 *baktun*s, 0 *katun*s, 0 *tun*s, 0 *uinal*s, 0 *kin*. That's why today's Maya name it Year Zero.

'On the third line, you've written how the new count of the thirteenth *baktun* will start with one *kin*, or one day. Now you know the answer to the strange messages that came on your printer and computer.'

'Yes, they're about the cycles of Time. They're giving the enigmatic Long Count dates for the 20th, 21st and 22nd December 2012, and the word EVOLOVE means that we 'evolve with love' on those dates!'

'Now I've solved the riddle for you. But don't ask me who sent them, unless you want me to tell you all about Time Spirit!'

'Perhaps I'll have to ask *Shangri-La* where those messages came from,' I mused. 'I no longer feel threatened by the internet or by the blog site I was using. It seems that, like people, computers can channel both good and bad. Like much of our modern technology, they can be used for positive or negative purposes.'

For clarity, the components of the Long Count are given as reference:

1 *kin*	= 1 day		
20 *kins*	= 1 *uinal*	=	20 days
18 *uinals*	= 1 *tun*	=	360 days
20 *tuns*	= 1 *katun*	=	7,200 days
20 *katuns*	= 1 *baktun*	=	144,000 days
13 *baktuns*	= 1 Great Cycle (5,200 *tuns*)	=	1,872,000 days

The Enigma of Time

I now set out to discover more about Time from Ken, a physicist friend. I began by reminding him of a simple statement made by Ray Cummings, a science fiction writer, in 1922: 'Time is what keeps everything from happening at once.'

'Well, yes, you could say that, but it's a bit more complicated now that science can explain everything,' said Ken, rather arrogantly, tweaking his ginger goatee beard and brushing lunch crumbs from his rather dated pink tie. Perhaps this was judgemental of me, but he looked a typical professor, pallid and pressured.

I said, 'Ken, I understand humans in the Palaeolithic era were using natural cycles of the Moon to calculate time, as early as 12,000, even possibly 30,000 BCE. Then science, religion and opinion all created a great divide between natural time, which is flowing and cyclical, and linear time. It has all become a great challenge to human thought processes, divided into time-counting – clocks – and time-charting – calendars.'

'Yes,' said Ken. 'The most precise time-counting devices of the ancient world were water clocks. One was found in the tomb of an Egyptian pharaoh, while Greeks, Chaldeans and later the Maya kept records of time as an essential part of their astronomical observations. Skilled Arab and Chinese inventors developed improved clocks in the Middle Ages.

'The first major advance in time-charting was by Julius Caesar, who introduced the solar-based Julian Calendar to the Roman empire in 45 BCE. It wasn't quite right because its intercalation still allowed astronomical solstices and equinoxes to advance against it by about eleven minutes per year.

'Pope Gregory XIII made a correction to this calendar in 1582, and his new Gregorian calendar was slowly adopted by different countries over a period of centuries. In Britain, for example, 2nd September 1752 suddenly became 14th September! While there are other major calendars, the Gregorian is the one in common use nowadays for business and practical purposes.'

I wanted to go deeper into Ken's knowledge of physics and time – not calendars. Dare I ask him about time travel? If I did, he would probably think me weird, but I knew that some astrophysicists were taking the possibility seriously. I decided to keep quiet for a bit as Ken went on talking. He was droning on about how accurate timekeeping is essential in the modern world.

Ken said authoritatively, 'Atomic clocks are accurate to seconds in many millions of years. Since 1967, the International System of Measurements has based its unit of time, the second, on the spinning properties of caesium atoms.'

'Yes, I have heard of atomic clocks, because it was reported that, after the approach of a comet in the mid-1990s and the dreadful Asian tsunami in 2004, they went wrong.'

'That's not quite right, Patricia,' insisted Ken. 'They didn't go wrong, but they sped up by a few milliseconds. It was all less than the blink of an eyelid, nothing to worry about.'

I'd had enough of his rather patronizing discourse and decided to take a risk with my question about time travel. I considered it would be too much for Ken if I mentioned the late Terence McKenna, an American author and futurist, who stood at the fringes of knowledge-seeking.

'So where does time travel come into all this?' I asked, trying to sound naïve.

Ken replied, 'In mainstream science, some have proposed that time travel could theoretically occur, but only into the future. It is much harder to rationally explain travel into the past.

'Now, listen carefully. Einstein's general theory of relativity explains that gravity slows time and that time runs faster in space where there is less gravitational pull. Other scientists investigating black holes, which incidentally they can't see, but only *think* are there, say that nothing, not even light, can escape from them. Time stands still in a black hole and, if you could by some scientific method just hover on the edge of a black hole, you would see all of Creation pass by in a twinkling of an eye. Then if you fell in, you would be beyond the End of Time.'

Beyond the End of Time? That sounded exciting to me. What else could I elicit from Ken?

'Einstein said that gravitation is a warping or distortion of space–time,' I said, seemingly knowledgably. 'What if a wormhole opened up? Couldn't you travel through it into different times?'

'No. That's science fiction. Such a thing could never happen.'

I had to counter this, even if he thought I was a fool. 'But what about the DARPA experiments that the USA supposedly instigated, and USS Eldridge, the ship that disappeared in the Philadelphia Experiment in October 1943? What about sightings of ghosts or flashbacks to past events that people have spontaneously experienced for centuries? Surely it's all something to do with the electromagnetic field and its interaction with the quantum field?'

'Look, I really don't know. They didn't teach me any of that at university. If you want to get involved in that sort of thing,' Ken said dismissively, but his face rapidly colouring to match his ginger goatee, 'I think you should look into a crystal ball.'

This was intended as a put-down. I hadn't got very far with Ken. Clearly he only wanted to talk about linear and Newtonian time.

Saying goodbye to Ken, I felt inexplicably excited, as if I was on to something big. I knew that superconsciousness and the quantum field *are* involved in our experience of Time. So, 'consult my crystal ball' was exactly what I did – though actually it was my time-travel crystal *Horus*, the same crystal I used in the *balché* ceremony. Over the years this crystal has taken me on time-travels into inner-space and, together with *Shangri-La*, the Himalayan skull, they made a powerful pair.

Time and the Cosmic Butterfly

I wanted to understand more, but not from a physicist's point of view. So I set up *Shangri-La* with *Horus* and began gazing deeply into the innermost part of the skull, searching for the magical in the mundane. I was looking into her heart, sensing her secrets.

Shangri-La reminded me that, within the connective quantum field revealed through the light of crystal skulls, magic is all around us. We only have to open our eyes, wake up, discard limiting cultural hypnosis and *see*. The realm of magic lies in a liminal space of transformation and transition, between what we experience as two segments of time, between what we see and what we don't see. I liken it to the opening and closing of a butterfly's wings.

When we glimpse this magic we are no longer trapped in our life-scenarios. We drop feelings of stress, our hearts and lungs expand, we breathe more easily and we are transformed. We experience opening, living lightly, singing the songs of Earth. While we each write our own songs, collectively we are stronger if we are with a choir of seekers. Our voices will be heard by the farthest stars when we sing in harmony, each precious note of our lives blending with each precious note of another.

When in the company of other like-minded souls, it encourages the renewal of our collective humanity. We seek this magic actively wherever we place our feet upon the Earth and open to Great Spirit, whose phenomenon of Time exists in order for us to come to know Eternity.

Holding *Shangri-La* and thanking her, I realized we are not short of what we endearingly call Time, but it is too vast for us to delay our spiritual growth a moment longer. It appears to speed up because we have forgotten that counting linear time is an illusion. The only real measure is spiral time, and this is what the ancient Maya knew about. This is why they are at the forefront of spiritual teachings today. Embedded deep in their culture are prophecies and messages that transcend Time. The Maya held Time up for us to look at, dissected it into twenty different calendars, moved it from *baktuns* (2,880,000 days) to *calabtuns* (1,152,000,000 days), and then threw it up in the air and asked, does Time matter anyway if it is an illusion?

Treading in the footsteps of the Maya, the author and visionary José Argüelles says we are 'in a Timequake, as the current 5,125 year long Time Beam nears completion'. This beam contains everything that has occurred in human history, as a vast store of holographic information. The beam is focused through the Sun, which has two aspects, the physical and the psychic.

Right now, Argüelles tells us we are at a stage of primitive planetary consciousness, but we are collectively waking up and moving from being physical beings to psychic beings. We are evolving because of the action of the Sun. The untold secret is that the ancient Maya knew that the Sun influences the telepathic power of the brain, because this is the method they used to ascertain when the current time period would begin (on 11th August, 3114 BCE) and when it would end.

They encoded crystal skulls and their cosmic teachings to remind us of this. According to Argüelles, our cosmic memory, held within the Akashic Field, is structured by a radial telepathic template that is holographic in nature. It transmits information instantaneously from one time–space to another and from one person to another. This is where the crystal skulls come in as informational receivers and transmitters to assist us. Hunbatz Men, the *hau'k'in*, in his simple English, explains, 'Crystal skulls activate the temples. They activate the human. Crystal skulls can help us do something better for humanity.'

We experience Time in many ways. We all know when it seems

to slow down or speed up. Commonly, Time fragments as we grow older and memory intrudes into the Now. This means that, in old age, we are neither befuddled nor inadequate, because we are preparing for timelessness – we are increasingly accessing the fractal, holographic nature of Time. Crystal skulls, whilst showing us *past* memories encoded within them, more importantly open perceptions of our *future symbolic self* that may choose our highest optimum path in life.

In this way we see that Time is not a measure of duration – it is a measure of change. It is a series of *nows*, out of which any future is possible. Hence there is no fixed future, only a choice to be made from multiple probabilities and futures. However, *collectively*, there are two major timelines spiralling before us. We can choose the positive path of evolutionary growth, or the path that traps us.

The magic in the mundane is visible if we deliberately step out of the ordinary frame of Time in which we appear to be trapped. We can look along our timelines to see the path of greatest probability. Because of the impact of free will, many possibilities may be woven into our futures.

So are we frequently limiting ourselves? What is the role of superconsciousness, as we learn to transcend Time? Many of the world's wisest teachers say 'look to thyself', because we attract and manifest what we need for our greatest soul-growth.

Although at this point I was trying to keep my focus upon the mystical aspects of Time, I couldn't help thinking of another view provided by science. A brilliant physicist, Brian Greene, professor and co-director of Columbia University's Institute for Strings, Cosmology and Astroparticle Physics (ISCAP), has simplified some very complex and controversial aspects of Time in his popular books such as *The Fabric of the Cosmos*. He began with some key questions: *is space a human abstraction, or is it a physical entity?* And, *what is reality?* or, more specifically, *what is space–time?*

Finally, when he asked *does time flow?* he dealt with special relativity. Special relativity means that observers moving relative to each other have different conceptions of what exists at any given moment – hence they have different conceptions of reality. His conclusion is that time does not flow, *as all things simultaneously exist at the same time.*

Aha! Rather a shamanic concept, I thought. But this is such a mind-boggling conundrum that it is better perhaps to break down our *perception* of space–time into small 'bites'. We can look at many aspects of space–time in this way: memory time–space, physiological time–space, psychic-mental time–space, psycho-mythic time–space, and planetary, stellar, universal and cosmic time-space.

Let me give you some examples. A *memory time–space* of long duration, as well as cosmic time–space, is encapsulated in the words of Marcus Aurelius, Roman emperor and philosopher, 121–180 CE, who stated, 'What we do in life ripples through eternity.'

Meanwhile, the words of Don Alejandro Cirillo Oxlaj Perez, spokesperson of the Council of the Maya, define a *psycho-mythic* time–space: 'The time of 13 *Ahau* and 13 *Baktun* is the time of the return of the ancestors and the men of wisdom.'

Maya researcher John Major Jenkins said of *psychic-mental* time–space: 'We are about to turn the corner and begin an ascending 13,000 year cycle, toward a new golden age of light and truth revealed. However, at this critical juncture the control systems and delusion-generating propaganda will be making a final effort to destroy life and consciousness on the planet.'

Joseph Campbell (1904–1987), the American mythologist and writer, succinctly summed up *planetary-cosmic* time–space: 'The goal of life is to make your heartbeat match the heartbeat of the universe, to match your nature with nature.'

These illustrations of time–space indicate that this is the moment – the *now* – when we must choose. The future is up to you and me, not only as individuals but collectively. We might be more connected than we once imagined.

I picked up *Shangri La*, holding her to my third eye chakra for better insight. What would the implication of these theories be, if they are correct? Would we know how to communicate instantly and over large distances? Would we have greater perceptions of unity? Would we inhabit a world of energies that mystics have been secretly describing for millennia? This immediate *knowing* is a recent development in the human race since, in the past, the majority of people were conditioned to live their lives through a fog of religious teachings.

I placed *Shangri La* next to *Horus* the timekeeper. Maybe what we will find, beyond all the scientific explanations, hidden within shamanic cosmovision, encapsulated in mythic stories, encoded within the crystal skulls, is a simple understanding as expressed by 19th-century English poet Francis Thompson, who wrote:

> All things, by immortal power,
> Near and far,
> Hiddenly
> To each other linked are,
> That thou canst not stir a flower
> Without troubling of a star.

.

CHAPTER THIRTEEN

The Evolution of Spiritual Consciousness

Father Sun, give me strength
Father Sun, make me wise
Father Son, make me into a seed
Father Son, make me Eternal.

– FROM *SOLAR MEDITATION* BY **HUNBATZ MEN**, COMUNIDAD
INDÍGENA MAYA, MEXICO

Crystal skulls are reminding us that, by being crystal clear in our thoughts, we are able to find the potential hidden within our own skulls, activated by our own hearts.

As individuals on an ascending life-path, there is work to be done regaining clarity, clearing out unneeded baggage or clutter in our lives. In these times of transition, we must push exploration of the phenomena of life and superconsciousness into deeper quantum realms. Humanity stands on stage watching and co-evolving a mystery whose players' consciousness will undergo a revival of inexplicable dimensions.

We can embody a higher consciousness, for this is superconsciousness. Although this state of mind was hinted at in ages past, it is being energized now as the unwritten but not unplanned super-sensory life, and light-encoded information activations play out in our familiar three-dimensional world.

Simultaneously, humanity is preparing to take an evolutionary leap of tangible physical changes brought about by realization of our oneness, into becoming a more advanced being – *Homo spiritus*. This epic event was not a reality even a century ago, when the famous Mitchell-Hedges skull was discovered. It is achievable now because we are entering the prophesied Year Zero, a new creation timeline of cosmo-mythic energy frequencies, heralded as the Maya Shift of the Ages.

A New Reality and Time-Spirit

Once again I visited the beautiful Maya city of Tulum. The last time I went there was to make an *ofrenda*, a simple altar giving thanks for my previous book *The Maya End Times*. Together with Mikhail, I took a leisurely stroll around the unique temples, just soaking up the special atmosphere. The scale of these temples is unusual, since they are very small in contrast to other Maya temples, which can take on monumental proportions.

I still hadn't worked out the reason for this, nor the reason why Tulum, set high on the cliffs above the Caribbean, is far and away my favourite place on Earth. Perhaps it is because of the tangible presence of the *aluxes*, little fairy-like spirits, or because of a real sense of timelessness as one looks far away across the intensely blue sea.

Mikhail and I sat in a small domed chamber near the Temple of the Rising Sun, alone except for the distant sound of breakers on the reef. We began talking about my current book – the memory of my previous *ofrenda* had perhaps given us both a sense of continuity. I felt the presence of the Nine Lords of Time very strongly.

Mikhail was guided to say, 'We modern humans are, from a western cosmological perspective in the Age of Aquarius, spiritual by natural influence for the ninth or birthing time, having undergone 97 astrological experiences out of the total of 144 for completion of the Earth experiment.'

I added, 'And, simultaneously, from a Maya cosmological perspective we are entering Year Zero and the Maya Fifth Creation.'

But Mikhail pointed out, 'We have been weighed down with Piscean Age baggage and the pollution of war. These need to be cleared from the land as well as from our minds. To regain clarity of purpose we can overcome mental clutter, which is really very insignificant compared to a visionary picture of life. At this point our human destiny, our very existence on Earth, is to understand and learn from the spiritual dimensions in the electromagnetic field *beyond time* and sourced *above the frequency of light*.

'We have been given intriguing insights. For example, we've learned that left-handed spin, polarized ultraviolet light from deep space, has determined the spin of DNA on Earth. This is an indicator of what we will soon be allowed to discover about the vibrational frequencies beyond light.'

I added, 'And within our bodies every cell and neuron uses a process governed by the speed of light, because thoughts move as a result of tiny photons of light making connections inside us.'

'Physically, we are living at the frequency of light. However, on Earth it's as if we've been tuned to the same radio station for the past 230,000 years, but so far we have not picked up the correct frequency for dynamic spiritual evolution. Now there is movement. Crystal-clear answers are coming to us through the medium of the skulls. They magnify ... they amplify in crystalline frequencies the aspirational thoughts of the world's visionaries.

Just imagine the power of thought created by one million people. Imagine the power of thought created by the world population of nearly seven billion people …' went on Mikhail.

I pointed out, 'The next human advancement will understand the vast potential of electromagnetic force-fields permeating the universe – even multi- or meta-verses. We will physically be unable to go out there, but electrically we will pass through the time barrier just as we passed through the sound barrier. Our vibrational energy-field will achieve this because we, All That Is, including crystal skulls and Time, are an intrinsic part of the same quantum field. As we have seen, we are all part of this great web of life, from the tiniest photon of light to a supernova.

'So the perspective revealed by the crystal skulls is that a facet of a co-creative impetus is awakening within us. It does not allow human thought processes to get in the way any longer. If you like to describe it thus, it is a mysterious new impulse from the spiritual world beyond our understanding, which is trying a fresh way to get into the human potential on this planet.'

'Let me explain how this has happened,' said Mikhail. 'Beginning with what I term Time-Spirit.'

'Can you explain exactly what that is?'

'In the same way as there is a physical, life-giving, energetic light and a spiritual element to Great Father Sun, so too there is a physical, life-giving and spiritual element to Time – or Time-Spirit. It holds accumulated past-life experiences, present experiences and future spiralling strands of time-possibilities on the Mat of Time, that we individually pull towards ourselves.'

'Yes, ongoing cycles of time, time-waves, were studied by the Maya in great depth in star observatories. They waited for the return of particular stars and planets that would bring their influences to bear upon the time-waves they so ardently entered in shamanic trance. Sculpting their arcane knowledge into stone, they reminded us that Time revolves in calendrical cycles of influence, albeit of a more intense frequency, higher or lower, as the spiral of the greater cosmic wave turns.'

Mikhail nodded. 'So what part in this mystery – for it is a mystery! – does the skull play?'

Shangri-La was 'lighting up', activating. I had become her full-time guardian because Soozie had given me her share, and the skull was very responsive to my thoughts. I answered, pointing: 'Look! See what is caused when attention is drawn to it. Emptying our minds of clutter leaves a space so that crystal skulls can "speak" inside our own skulls, asking us, 'Haven't you got our message yet?'

'When we encounter crystal skulls we soon move past exclamations of beauty, fascination or even spookiness. Skulls remind us of death and we do indeed need to face death, but death as a sacred initiation in order to be lifted to a new level of being. In our exploration of crystal skulls we have gone way beyond any fear of death. We have journeyed into superconsciousness and flowed with Time-Spirit onto distant shores of the universe, as we explored a limitless quantum sea of life and light revealed through them.' I paused, looking deeply into *Shangri-La*.

'We are beginning to see new faculties of perception emerging. Through that emergence a new language, a new song, of spiritual light from Time-Spirit will be shaped. Crystal skulls are helping us to evolve in this way, sharpening up our perceptions, making us crystal-clear.'

Reluctantly we left the Tulum temples and returned to our friend's house nearby. It gave an opportunity to read what Kathleen Murray, crystal skull guardian, had said. She summed up many of my own conclusions:

The role of crystal skulls today is to empower humanity to remember their divine origins. They now, as in the past, store cosmic memory, which assists in souls' missions. They send out codes which awaken the 'spiritual brain' we all have.

There is no separation between humanity's consciousness and that of crystal skulls. It is more like two different incarnational forms of the same consciousness. We are all from the stars. We are all great beings who form light into matter. We have the power to manifest our love and create our dreams and our realities.

They are our stellar family, our brothers and sisters from the stars. They are us and we are they. They are here to remind us of the divinity we are. It is a mutual journey to remember and bring into wholeness all aspects of ourselves which have lost the freedom to love.

There are crystal skulls on this planet which will always live inside the Earth. There is no need for humans to 'find' them. There are others whose journey is to assist human beings to awaken and understand their legacies and heritage.

There are so many active crystal skulls working with their guardians now in all their different ways, it is an inspiring time! It is great pleasure to have such loyal companions.

There will always be, as there always have been, Dreamers' Skulls, Skulls of Record and Magicians' Skulls, which were, and are, always very distinctive.

By awakening the crystal skulls, humanity awakens itself.

We are remembering. We are awakening.

Crystal skulls are showing us other levels of reality. They enable us to put aside materialistic distractions, clarify our highest intentions and expand concepts of what our consciousness really is, and what this means to us individually and collectively. We are discovering that insects and trees, fishes and snakes all have a part to play, so in the interdependence of all life and the biodiversity of our planet we will find more answers. The ancestors and beings who communicate through the skulls are also priming us, carbon-based beings that we are, to take on innovative silicon-based knowledge. Together they are singing out their messages, loud and clear.

The significance of this new expansive superconscious reality is flowing on the waves of Time-Spirit, washing us towards the shores of a new paradigm. We are riding the planetary wave into extraordinary new dimensions of spiritual energy and insights, for we are birthing a new age of humanity, the realization of a 230,000-year plan within a Great Cycle of Time.

Already some amongst us are engaging with the new adventure in human consciousness ebbing and flowing over our planet. We are in the ninth Platonic Aquarian Age and, like the ninth month of birth, the power is unstoppable. This is the wave of evolution through illumination of *Homo sapiens sapiens* into *Homo sapiens spiritus*, that is about to break on our shores.

Riding the Wave

You may well ask, how do I know if I am tapping into super-consciousness and the enigmatic waves of Time-Spirit? Well, you will experience one or all of the following.

You will experience increased intuition or 'hunches'. You'll come to understand that what is meant to be will happen in its own time. You will have taken on Gebser's adage, 'You are what you think'. You will have a heightened awareness of or sensitivity to your surroundings, and you'll have enhanced creative thinking, using the right side of the brain, with increased receptivity to new positive ideas.

You will experience more synchronicities in everyday life,

empathy with other people and deeper levels of compassion or 'heart-centred' unconditional love. You will respond more positively to nature, including all Earth's creatures. You'll find increased group consciousness with family, friends and colleagues, with an encompassing sense of unity that moves beyond the mental polarities of black–white, good–bad, and you'll feel that unity as a peaceful collective quantum awareness. You will engage with new-paradigm energy technologies and quantum healing modalities. You will honour the environment of the Earth and all her peoples.

Here we see the workings of Time-Spirit. It is an intrinsic, indivisible part of the superconsciousness dimension. It is the integral reality and non-local consciousness of the Akashic Field (Ervin Lazlo's term) or Morphic Field (Rupert Sheldrake's term). What it means is that we are all co-creators of our own realities. It enables us to transcend limiting egos and earthbound *karma*, the archaic law of 'cause and effect'. We are becoming illuminated beings, attuned to a flowing cosmos.

The simple personal insights of Time-Spirit mean that we are joyous and blessed by the way each day blossoms. We value the *now*-moment and are more attuned to higher guidance, awareness and healing. We may develop an ability to hear or see beyond our usual human range, experiencing clairaudience and clairvoyance. We will be able to enter reflective and meditative states at will, becoming a fractal and holistic part of the great mystery of human evolution.

Along the way we each reclaim our inheritance to heal ourselves and others, because faultless connectivity exists everywhere, from outer space to within the cells of our bodies. Yet Time-Spirit speaks of one other all-important message. It concerns our inner life of soul and spirit, making a part of that visible through light. It is the expansion of human potential that mystics throughout the ages have hinted at. Organized religions have tried to engender this but largely they have failed. Today we stand, metaphorically, on the edge of the abyss – we can fall or fly. If we fly, and shamanically this is a valid description, we pass beyond the barrier of Time. We engage with the enigma of Time by entering the inner realms where we discover 'innerscape-ability'.

In the inner realms, what we consider to be real changes. 'Reality' becomes infinitely flexible and sacred in every moment. We don't lose our individuality when we engage with our innerscape-ability, for we are the co-creators of both the inner and the outer worlds.

We human beings are able to enter the darkness to find the light within, and we can reclaim our cosmic connection to illumination.

Shangri-La

The following day Mikhail and I were back at Tulum. Sitting together on a stone bench built into the wall of the temple that greets the rising sun, we reviewed this book.

'Alloa Patricia, I bet you would have asked different questions of the crystal skull guardians, knowing what you know now,' said Mikhail, challengingly.

'Not at all,' I responded, placing *Shangri-La* carefully on my lap and giving Mikhail the time-travel crystal *Horus* to hold. 'You remember my questions, don't you? They were, *What has been the role of crystal skulls in the past and what is their role today?, What is the connection between 'ancient' Central American and Himalayan crystal skulls? and, In what ways are the crystal skulls connected with the evolution of spiritual consciousness?*

'Well, if I could have picked up a crystal ball right at the beginning of this adventure, seeking a vision of the future, I couldn't have wished for a better outcome. The crystal skulls have prompted me to look deeply into my own skull. In some curious way, they have taught me how to really *love* the Earth and all her peoples.'

I paused, enjoying the warmth of Great Father Sun permeating the ancient stones at my back. Looking far across the azure sea, to where our wise teachers say the Maya race originated in Atlantis within the misty cauldron of the past, I continued …

'I discovered many connections between East and West, the shift of spiritual consciousness in earlier times and what is happening today. I made a tangible connection with the Lords of Time and the enigma of what may unfold. Then the skulls revealed, with your help – and the tortillas! – the critical position in which Earth and humanity stand as we enter the Platonic ninth month of birth that coincides with so many predictions, and especially with those of the Maya Year Zero.'

'And what of the thirteen crystal skulls?' asked Mikhail.

'What I have discovered, that also strikes a chord with Hopi teachings, is that they will only be fully activated when human life has sunk to a really low ebb. Yet, as that culminates, a critical mass of people will rise up who will choose positivity over negativity. That somehow makes sense to me. A clearing and a cleansing has to occur before healing and a new peace-loving humanity can emerge to cherish the Earth.

'The golden crystal skull inside my head has shown me the intricacies of Time and caused me to use superconsciousness to probe into the quantum energy-field. It has urged me to link my head, my inner sacred pyramid, with my heart, and it has shown me unlimited love. Do you remember the two choices humanity has to make on the timelines? Between the one that keeps us trapped in cultural hypnosis and the one that promises a positive future and an evolution into spiritually evolved beings.'

'Very well,' responded Mikhail.

'I know which one I will choose!'

On our last few evenings in Mexico we went down to the wooden jetty at Puerto Morelos, close to Tulum, which provides a mooring for fishing boats. As Great Father Sun dips below the roofs of the town, the boats return full with their catch. Accompanied by the familiar outlines of black frigate birds in the sky, they arrive under the watchful eyes of up to a dozen large pelicans. As the fish are cleaned and filleted there is a fierce aerial combat for scraps thrown into the sea. What the birds don't get sinks down in the water, attracting scores of small fish.

I pointed out to Mikhail two ghostly grey shadows that suddenly materialized. They were manta rays, as large as tables, with long whip tails. They glided effortlessly in the shallow water and, like vacuum cleaners, devoured the smaller fish. *What an example of the interdependence of life!* I thought. A food chain in action. But the manta rays too, now a 'near-threatened' species through over-fishing, could become food and sport for the many harpoon hunters that are attracted to the coral reef some 700m offshore.

Mikhail and I had been coming to this remaining unspoilt stretch of coast for years. Sadly it is now sandwiched between a nature reserve endeavouring to preserve turtle nesting grounds and mushrooming developments of expensive 'condos' and self-styled 'eco-lodge hotels'. We would miss the morning fly-past of pelicans, the soft white sand and refreshing margaritas served in glasses as big as fishbowls!

I held tightly onto *Shangri-La* as we watched the fishermen. What a lot of beautiful wisdom she had taught me. It was time to really *remember* who I was by releasing my crystal skull – in effect to recycle her energy as nature here had shown.

Mikhail and I decided we would sleep the night on the soft sandy beach beneath the stars, with the skull between us. Looking up, we saw the Milky Way and the turtle of Orion in the sky.

I remembered the beginning of my quest in Spain in the cave of the ancestors' skulls, that led eventually to my travels in China and the Mayalands. Along the way I learned about crystal skulls, the quantum universe and the enigma of Time.

I had realized that I shouldn't rely on computers and the internet to be the replacement for Truth. And one of the lessons of this quest was to find and work with my own innerscape-ability of superconsciousness, following wherever that would take me. In my heart I was appreciative that so much had been shared with us by the crystal skull guardians and the Maya elders. I wanted to give something back by way of sacrifice.

Setting in motion a sacrifice redoubles the effect of a ceremony and literally means 'offering a sacred face'. Mikhail reminded me that, in very ancient burials, a mask was sometimes placed on the skull with the specific intention of communicating into the afterlife. Sacrifice is something intended to be taken seriously, a real commitment, a rite of passage to remember. It bridges this world and Creation. It was 9 *K'at* (9 *Kan*) the primary day to make 'payment' to our ancestors. Nine signifies completion.

As Great Father Sun's golden orb was about to rise in the sky, Mikhail and I carried *Shangri-La* into one of the fishing boats. We asked the skipper to go just a few kilometres along the coast and anchor where we could see the exquisite solar temples of Tulum.

It was time to say goodbye.

> The Dew is on the lotus! – Rise, Great Sun!
> And lift my leaf and mix me with the wave.
> Om mani padme hum, the sunrise comes!
> The dewdrop slips into the shining sea!
>
> – From 'The Light of Asia', a poem by Sir Edwin Arnold,
> presenting the life and teachings of Buddha.

·

Days in the Maya Calendar and an Introduction to Maya Time

By Mikhail, Solar Initiate and Co-Director of the Sun & Serpent Maya Mysteries School, UK and Spain.

Imagine being in time and space without a calendar to remind you of Thanksgiving Day, Labour Day, Christmas or bank holidays. Picture what your construct of time might be.

In the past, long before the Gregorian calendar began, the Maya learnt from Father Sun, Sister Moon and Mother Earth that mankind is a sacred being. They marked time with calendars to create order for a human being's life, from conception to death. One of them specifically connects with the right to inhabit Mother Earth with responsibility. This traditional calendar is called *Cholq'ij* in Kiché Mayan (*T'zolk'in* in Yucatec Mayan).

In this calendar two specific aspects are respected: the divine law of the Creator and the natural law on the Earth, by which we move through time and space, based upon a 260-day cycle – 260 days was chosen for a number of reasons, including the pre-birth time spent in our mothers' wombs.

Using its guidance presents a model to live by, providing a

weave of divinatory possibilities and, most importantly, offering a way to respect yourself, your family, your community and all that lives, stands and grows on Mother Earth. Additionally this calendar embraces honouring eldership during one's 52nd year of life.

Below are introductory words giving an idea of the value placed upon each of the twenty day-symbols of the calendar, and how they may be used interpretively. The day names are given first in Kiché and then in Yucatec Mayan. Should you choose to use this calendar, please respect its origins, remembering that thirteen numbers interweave with twenty names. Guatemalan tradition includes invoking day names during fire ceremonies, in order to honour and give 'payment' to Mother Earth. You may choose to allow the words to guide your actions to connect with spiritual aspects of time.

To discover today's Mayan date, go to: www.dr-rock.biz/MayanDateCalculator.html or http://www.diagnosis2012.co.uk/conv.htm

IMOX = Imix
The spirit of rain. Communication with water animals, dolphins, whales and crocodiles. The day to settle and make order to balance mess and chaos. A day to connect with development and evolution of the world and humanity; strength of our minds. Maintaining unity of all ideas and setting within ourselves a positive and centred balance.

IQ = Ik
Day of the Spirit of the Air, representing wind and breath. Clouds, travelling in the sky. Lightning and storms. Nutrition.

AQ'AB'AL = Akbal
A day of a new era, a new lasting life. Dawn, sunrise. Getting

clearer, awakening. Keeping away confusion and ignorance. A day to evaluate darkness and light.

K'AT = Kan

A day to make 'payment' to our ancestors. Strength and warmth in our hearts, from our Creator. A day to solve complicated matters, to make friends, to form the union of a group or society and to ask for unity in the whole community. The web, the knots and the problems which lodge in us.

KAAN = Chicchan

A strong day with strength and the power of the snake. The force of the universe, linking the Heart of the Sky with the Heart of the Earth. A day to recognize agility, the wisdom of the elders, sincerity, balance, power and authority.

KAME = Cimi

A day to pardon all the evil actions committed. Dissolution of all good and bad things. Death. To examine harmony, vision, smartness and intelligence. It forecasts good and evil. It means dying and being born, further dimensions, the big change! The continuation of life for children.

KEJ = Manik

This day is highly positive, concerned with the destiny of humanity. A day to have special regard to the four strengths of Mother Nature which nourish life: Sun, Earth, Air, Water. Pay special regard to be in service with humility on this day. Petition for solidarity and stability as well as for the four-leggeds. A day for examining the authority of village or community. The vision of what is to come.

Q'ANIL = Lamat

The day to acknowledge and work with regeneration of the Earth, with rebirth after death. The day to focus on growth of the sacred corn, vitality, fertility of human beings, animals and plants. It symbolizes the four colours of corn (yellow, red, black and white) and the cosmic seed planted on this planet.

TOJ = Muluc

The day of payment to Creation, to Mother Earth, to the Universe and to all the elements. Paying for the benefits and challenges presented in our life. The day of the sacred ceremonial fire and giving offerings for a just balance, settlement of love, communication or renewal.

TZ'I = Oc

The day of the dog, which gives help and advice. A special day to focus on energy in natural places like altars or pyramids. The essence of this day speaks about law, authority, justice, faithfulness and order. It is the day for the protector of both material and spiritual laws.

B'ATZ' = Chuen

B'atz' is time in motion and evolution, infinite time, spirituality, the creator of life and wisdom. A day to work with evolution and human life. *B'atz'* rules marriage. It represents continuity with the past. The strength of the weavers.

EE = Eb

The path. The journey. The day of the personality and material goods. The guide and protector of traders. Many aspects of the path – the beginning of a labour, a trip, a journey. It is the sacred White Path, the development of life.

AJ = Ben

It is the day of renewal, purification and rebirth and to give thanks for shelter and the family. A day to make payment for integrity, honesty and rightness. The Day of the Sacred Bundle. A day to work with the seven virtues (fire, water, air, land, Heart of the Sky, Heart of the Earth and the centre) of the divine power, the sacred words, love towards humanity, as well as unexpected dreams.

I'X = Ix

Day of the Jaguar or the Four Balaams, and understanding flexibility of the feline, the feminine part. It represents the Mayan altar and sacred places. The day of the mountains, summits and plains. It is the day of High Magic: this energy develops the superior powers, intermediary between real and unreal.

TZ'IKIN = Men

The day of the birds, carriers of good luck. It is the day of communication with the Heart of the Sky and the Heart of the Earth, symbolizing good fortune, luck and material stability. It is the intermediary between the Creator/Builder and the human being. The vision is panoramic, like the eagle.

AJMAQ = Cib

The day of moral strengths. The day when people asked for forgiveness of Mother Earth for all the mistreatment and abuses brought upon her by people. Thanking Mother Earth for the benefits provided by her. *Ajmaq* is a day of profound, deep thoughts.

NO'J = Caban

The day of connection between the spiritual Cosmic Mind and the human mind, when ideas and wisdom may emerge, and mental speed and smartness are sought. Nobility is the major virtue and in particular patience and prudence may be petitioned. It is the day of decision-taking and of advice.

TIJAX = Etznab

The day of healers and doctors. It is the sign of strong, brave and courageous persons, who collaborate, who are friendly and loving. It reflects flexibility in space and time. It is the cutting, separation, the knife for healing and harmonizing the four bodies (physical, mental, emotional, spiritual). The knife of obsidian stone means strength, power of the warrior, the radical, the revelation through quick and varied images. Obsidian is the mirror which reflects our soul.

KAWOQ = Cauac

The day of the mediators, defenders, judges. The day of the woman who warms up the heart of the home with her maternal love. Guardian energy for the wellbeing and security of all. It is the day of the energy of nature and the elements. A beneficial day for the village or community to work towards the same goal.

APU = Ahau

The day of the spiritual warrior. Spiritual awakening. This sign bears material and spiritual certainty. It is the transformation and mutation, the one who carries out miracles. Honouring the Sun. The day of greatness and strength of life. It is the intervention of the ancestors responding to the requests made during a ceremony. It represents the physical strength to go on living after death.

·

Quartz Crystal Properties

Quartz is the mineral name for the chemical silicon dioxide (silica and oxygen), and is one of numerous silicate minerals to be found within the Earth's crust. Quartz usually has recognizable crystals with six 'faces' or a six-sided prism ending in a six-sided pyramid. It is found in varying sizes and many different colours, ranging through pink, golden, blue, green, red or smoky grey, and sometimes has inclusions of other minerals within it.

Modern technology artificially grows crystals of silicon metal, the silicon chips that are used in computers. Other laboratory crystals are quartz for the electronics industry, ruby crystals for lasers, industrial diamonds and sapphires for bearings.

Quartz has many properties, including polarization, reception, reflection, refraction, magnification, transduction, amplification, focusing, transmutation, transference, transformation, storage, capacitance, stabilization, modulation, balancing and transmittance. It has a hexagonal structure made of trigonal or rhombohedral crystals. Quartz has been discovered in meteorites and Moon rocks.

Its piezo-electrical properties are well known to scientists. By directing electricity through quartz there is an alternating expansion and contraction in the crystal structure, of a vibration at a particular frequency. In quartz watches a tiny slice of synthetic quartz receives electricity from a battery. The frequency of vibration is then counted by a tiny computer and, because the rate at which the slice of crystal vibrates is known to the manufacturers, it serves as a timekeeper.

On the gem scale of hardness, quartz is just below diamonds. Modern cutting processes use a diamond-impregnated blade to saw a lump of crystal or gemstone into the rough shape required, which is then ground down on lapping wheels. Lapidaries (gem cutters) say that quartz crystal is fairly easy to carve, compared to jade which is ten times more likely to shatter.

However, many crystal skull researchers state that metal tools were not used to carve ancient skulls because telltale microscopic marks do not occur on them. Sometimes they suggest diamonds were employed but, as diamonds are brittle as well as hard, they easily shatter if used as a tool. A more likely explanation is that ancient crystal skull carvers first chipped (cobbed) pieces off a block of material that was destined to be shaped into a skull. Then they might have cut the stone more precisely with a 'mud saw', using tightly strung hemp fibre or fire-hardened bamboo. Next, fine work would have been done by sand bow drills, using a fine slurry of sand as a grinding medium and finished by polishing with different grades of sand. Such methods are still commonly used for drilling holes in beads and ornaments.

.

Himalayan/Mongolian/Chinese Crystal Skulls

L ionFire (David R Leonard), USA, is a gateway for many of the most ancient stone and crystal skulls coming out of Mongolia. His work with these skulls has given him international recognition as one of the world's major crystal skull-keepers.

I am indebted to him for being able to work with the following when he came to Glastonbury, UK, in 2008: a skull, Tzo'La, of green and yellow leopard jade, Legendary Period, 3500 to 0 BCE, Northeast River District of Inner Mongolia; a clear obsidian skull with a Bat Totem carved on the cranium, early Historic Period, Inner Mongolia; and *Ku*, red jade, authenticated to be early Neolithic, 5000 BCE, from ancient ceremonial areas in the Northeast River District of Inner Mongolia.

LionFire has kindly contributed the following information in this section.

Introduction

It has long been thought that the artistic styles of some ancient Maya groups mirror oriental line language and iconic imagery. Many oriental groups migrated to the New World, bringing much of their culture, ritual and art with them, including the making and use of crystal and stone skulls in ceremony. These oriental groups may have brought some of their ancient crystal skulls with them to the New World.

New archaeological evidence has now proven that matriarchal, Goddess-based, semi-nomadic tribes roamed the area between Himalayan Tibet and Mongolia. These ancient Neolithic people were the first to begin carving stone into objects of both utility and art. By approximately 10000 BCE they began to carve stones and crystals into skulls.

Himalayan Origins: Ancient Times

The Tibetan, Mongolian and Chinese civilizations span a vast expanse of time, from 20000 BCE (Palaeolithic) to the present. These civilizations are a miracle of human creativity and civilization. The Culture of Jade is closely linked to the development of Central Asia, and Confucius said, 'A gentleman is judged by the quality of his jade.' Not only was jade more valuable than gold, but the design of jade wares varied according to social status.

The oldest jade ware discovered dates back to 8000+ years ago. It is a jade dagger excavated at the Relic Pyramid of Hu in Shanxi province. The largest pieces of jade-stone carving took ten years for the artists of Yangzhou to complete. Some of these early pieces are on display at the British Museum, London.

The Neolithic culture, from 8000 to 4500 BCE, is one of the earliest and most advanced civilizations discovered to date, in China. This culture was located mainly in the land area between Inner Mongolia and present day Liaoning and Hubei provinces – new evidence reveals possible settlements in the Yangtze River area as well.

These Jade People were the Goddess-based, matriarchal, semi-nomadic, shamanic cultures that consisted of several tribal groups located between the western Liaohe river valley, the Dalinghe river valley and the northern bank of Bohai Bay, south of Yanshan mountain. These tribes that pre-date the Liang Zhu period have not been officially named and are referred to only as late Neolithic – 6500 to 4500 BCE.

Many of their ancient sites are newly discovered, due to a large Chinese government dam and infrastructure project that has now flooded and destroyed these ancient ceremonial centres that were used for over 6,500 years and contain hundreds of thousands of tombs. Artefacts from these tombs and ceremonial areas span many ages and style changes from the oldest (8000 BCE) to the most recent from the historic era, beginning around 1 CE). *Carved skulls are found in nearly every tomb that has been excavated.*

The Niuheliang site in the Northeast River District belongs to the late period of the Liang Zhu Culture, 3500 BCE. The ancient shamanic people were temple, pyramid and city builders who created some of the earliest nephrite jade and stone carvings. Their sophisticated carving techniques employed technologies that exceed simple explanations. The largest crystal and stone skulls were found in these ceremonial centres.

Many of the skulls are made from jade, obsidian, agate, turquoise or quartz and other crystal. They are well preserved due to the fact that this culture utilized slab burial tombs and because of the arid climate of Inner Mongolia. Other materials used, from the Liang Zhu into the late Legendary Period, included stained magnasite, lapis lazuli, carnelian and blue-green, gold and red obsidian. Stones were often dyed and stained using mineral compounds including iron, ochre, cinnabar, copper and silver solutions.

It has recently been discovered that these late Neolithic artists possessed the knowledge of metallurgy and employed the use of copper and iron tools to work their jade masterpieces. The practice of mineral staining and dyeing stone began about 3500 BCE, once metallurgy was introduced to or discovered by these societies.

Many artefacts show the use of saw blades and drilling instruments, reflecting the fact that they were a highly technologically advanced civilization. Currently, there is no known artefact evidence, from any other Neolithic cultures in the world, showing that metal tools were used to shape jade during this very early Neolithic era. Bronze was brought to China by the easternmost Caucasians living in the mid-hinterlands between Europe and Asia. It is the opinion of master-teacher Wong Tien Chung that these ancient people extracted iron ore and nickel alloys from meteorites to make ritual jade shaping tools to carve the stone and crystal skulls.

Chinese archaeologists have recently discovered a late-Neolithic pyramid-shaped building dating back more than 5,500 years in the Inner Mongolia Autonomous Region, in north China. It is similar to the much later Maya pyramids of Central America. This discovery sheds light on the fact that the ancient shamanic Mongolian tribes were one of the first people known to have built pyramid and temple structures.

Ancient jade ritual and art objects were created for a period of more than 8,000 years. Neolithic jades have been discovered in large quantities with over 52 different types of jade objects in various shapes and forms, including ceremonial wands and blades, dragons, goddesses, sexual tools, skulls, spines, full skeletons, totem animals and jewellery.

Another fascinating observation through the study of ceremonial jade artefacts is the abundance of alien-like motifs and figurines that are completely unexplainable, as they are not found in other Neolithic cultures. It is obvious from the study of Inner

Mongolian sacred sites that there was a highly sophisticated knowledge of mathematics and astronomy which is evident by the celestial alignments of their pyramids, platform mounds and ceremonial structures.

The extensive employment of ritual jades in China by the shaman-priests during its late prehistory must certainly demonstrate to the world of archaeology that these people were not Neolithic Age but rather Jade Age people. It is believed that these tribes were actually the Xinglongwa people who migrated into China from Mongolia when global weather conditions turned their rich forested world into desert. New discoveries reveal that the Xinglongwa people had sophisticated jade carving techniques over 8,500 years ago. The lost historic trails of these great people are waiting to be discovered. Perhaps they were descendants from a long lost and advanced civilization.

Ancient jade artefacts are gemstone treasures from the distant past that have withstood the tests of both time and humanity. Most have been buried for centuries, while others may have been buried for several millennia. The condition of each ancient jade artefact varies depending on the age, the type of earth the artefact was buried in and the geological conditions that surrounded the jade artefact.

Most ancient jades form a crust of calcification that is deposited in layers upon the gem's original surface during its burial. When an ancient jade is dug up, it often has its original colours hidden by layers of soil, minerals and encrustations, including calcium, ochre, cinnabar, sulphur and iron. Almost all jade artefacts dug from the earth have these layers of encrustations removed by scientists, to reveal the gemstone's original colours and characteristics or to catalogue any totems, glyphic designs or writing they may possess. These new discoveries have opened the door for many of these treasures (stone and crystal skulls and spiritual tools), to become available to the public as a way to fund further research.

The most ancient jade skulls and spiritual tools were made from the outer areas of jade deposits, which are considered very poor quality stone. It wasn't until later times that the purer, more brightly-coloured jades, from deeper in the jade veins, was used.

When you hold an ancient jade artefact in your hands and you marvel at its age and its message, then you'll begin to understand that the journey down the 'Jade Road' is a journey of a thousand lifetimes.

The collecting of river jade was concentrated in the White Jade (Yurungkash) and Black Jade (Karakash) rivers of the Yarkand. On the southern leg of the Silk Road, yearly tribute payments consisting of the most precious white jade were made to the Chinese imperial court. Serpentine jade or Xiu jade is mainly from Xiuyan county in Liaoning Province. Made of many different ingredients, it takes on various appearances and colours. Serpentine jade is usually semi-transparent or opaque, like wax.

From the earliest Chinese dynasties until the present, the jade deposits in most use were from the region of Hetian in the western Chinese province of Xinjiang. Hetian jade was used to create many utilitarian and ceremonial objects, ranging from indoor decorative items to jade burial suits. White and greenish Hetian jade is found in small quarries and as pebbles and boulders in rivers.

Lantian jade was mined in Lantian County, north of Xian in Shaanxi province. It was also among the most charming of ancient jades, for its rigidity and fine grain made it easier to be carved into decorations and jewellery by the shaman artists. The hue is uneven in colours of yellow or light green.

Nanyang jade: Henan province is famous for its abundant Nanyang, Dushan jade. It is distinctive for its whimsical colour layering. Among the Nanyang jade artworks are rare purple, blue and red colours.

Jadeite (Burma Fei Cui jadeite) was brought into China during the early Qing Dynasty (1644–1911). Jadeite contains an iron component which turns it red, or chromium which turns it yellow. Jadeite can also be green and many other colours. Known as 'gemstone jade' or the 'king of jade', it is usually much more expensive than other varieties.

Dong Ling jade is referred to as aventurine in the west, and green quartz in Brazil.

LionFire is a shamanic practitioner, healer and reiki master. He is a professional, multi-faceted artist, ceremonialist and performer in a variety of media, currently working with many Maya shamans.

APPENDIX FOUR List of Crystal Skulls

Name of skull	Type of crystal	Name of guardian	Age & origin (if known)	Other information
Alexander	Aventurine	Grandfather Tue Bear	Unknown	Deceased. Present guardian unknown
Amakua	Bluish Quartz	Star Johnsen-Moser, USA	Ancient: Himalayan	Found in cave, via Frank Loo
Amar	Quartz	crystalskulls.com	Old: Tibetan	22lbs. One of the largest skulls
Ami	Amethyst	Private collectors, USA	Ancient: C America	8.5lbs. Ex-president Porfiro collection?
AsKaRa	Jadeite	Kathleen Murray & Gillian Ellis, UK	2200-3500 BCE or Lemurian	Tibetan? Or Liangzhu? Full skeleton
Bat Totem Skull	Clear Black Obsidian	LionFire, USA	Early historic period	Inner Mongolia
Beijing Skulls	Quartz & various	Unknown	Old or Ancient. China	Group of 22 skulls & Dropa discs
Berlin / Gestapo Skull	Quartz	Possibly in Vatican	Unknown	According to IKA, a very negative skull
Bob	Quartz & rainbows	Cece Stevens	Unknown	5lbs. Purchased Tucson, USA
Bolormaa	Quartz	Sue Kitts	Old. Mongolia	Mongolian, via Frank Loo
British Museum	Quartz	Dept Ethnology, London	Ancient or Old	In museum since 1898
Cana-Ixim	Green Jade	crystalskulls.com	Ancient / Old Maya. Guatemala	4lbs. Found in cave. Has glyphs on cranium
Chuen	Smoky Quartz	Wendy Willett, UK	Said to be Venus	Monkey-like

Table continues

Name of skull	Type of crystal	Name of guardian	Age & origin (if known)	Other information
Compassion	Quartz on matrix	Joseph Bennett	Old or Ancient	Moveable jawbone, comparable to M-Hedges
Eh ha Y U	Quartz	Shavat Y, N'lands/Mexico	Old	
Einstein	Quartz	Carolyn Ford, USA	Ancient or Old. Large skull	33lbs. 4 crystals fit perfectly into its eyes
ET	Smoky Quartz	Joky Van Dieten, Netherlands	Ancient or Old. Guatemala	4.99kg. Found 1906. Pointed cranium
Geronimo	Smoky Quartz	Joshua Shapiro, USA	Modern	2lb. Full name: Geronimo Golden Eagle Eye
Grandmother Rainbow	Quartz	DaEl Walker, USA	C America	
Heruka	Quartz. Decorated	Harishyam, USA	Old. Ali province, Tibet	Gift to Buddhist family by monks, 100 years ago
Jade	Nephrite Jade	Kathleen Murray, Scotland	Ancient, 10,000+ years	Mongolian, from a temple. 4.5kg.
Jomcata Mayab	Quartz	Lia Scallon, Australia	Modern, Brazil	600gms
Kalif	Smoky Quartz	Kathleen Murray, Scotland	Modern, China	15 cm high, 6kg. Elestial crystals inside
Ku	Red Jade	LionFire, USA	Early Neolithic, 5000 BCE	NE River District, Inner Mongolia
Kuun Ti Tsin	Amethyst	Private collector, Germany	Old. Central America	14.22lbs. Excavated from a tomb. Large skull
Leopard Jade	Leopard Jade	LionFire, USA	Legendary period	Inner Mongolian. 12lbs
Liaoning Skulls	White / yellow / green	Unknown	Old. China	Group of unearthed 'screaming' skulls
Luv	Rose Quartz	Joky Van Dieten, Netherlands	Russia. Scythian culture?	Found in a burial mound

Table continues

Name of skull	Type of crystal	Name of guardian	Age & origin (if known)	Other information
Madre	Smoky Quartz	Laurie Walker, USA	Ancient	5 ins high. 11lbs. Round face
Mahasamatman	Quartz	Kathleen Murray, Scotland	Extraterrestrial	12 cm high. 1.5kg
Marin Skull	Amethyst	Unknown, in USA	Old or Ancient Mayan	Unearthed 1900s. Studied by N Nocerino
Max, 'Texas Skull'	Quartz	JoAnn Parks, USA	Ancient. Guatemala	Once in care of a Tibetan healer-monk
Maya	Clear Quartz	Jane Doherty, USA	Old. Central America. 4+lbs	Purchased 1987, Mexico. Three rows of teeth.
Maya Skull	Clear Quartz	Unknown, in USA	Old or Ancient Mayan	8.7lbs. Unearthed 1900s. Studied by N Nocerino
Mitchell-Hedges	Quartz	Bill Homann, USA	Ancient. Lubuntuun, Belize	'Skull of Love'. Moveable jawbone
Naga K'u	Himalayan Quartz	Hunbatz Men, Mexico	Old	Presented to Hunbatz Men Oct 2009
Nefertiti	Chevron Amethyst	DaEl Walker, USA	Ancient	Elongated skull
Octagona	Quartz	Karlos E Ah Puch, Mexico	Unknown	
Orisa	Black Obsidian	Joanne V Wijgerden, Netherlands	Unknown	5.6lbs
Pancho	Quartz	Mario Bojorquez, USA	Old or Ancient. Monte Alban	Hollow. 10in tall. 13 lbs. Zapotec or Atlantean
Paris Skull	Cloudy Quartz	Musée du Quai Braly, Paris	Old, possibly Aztec	11cm high. 2.75kg. Vertical hole
Portal de Luz	Smoky Quartz	Joshua Shapiro, USA	Modern, Brazil, 1998	10lbs, but apparently weight and colour change
Rainbow	Quartz	DaEl Walker, USA	Ancient or Old. Guerro, Mexico	5.9lbs. Excavated 1995

Table continues

Name of Skull	Type of crystal	Name of guardian	Age & origin (if known)	Other information
Reliquary Cross	Quartz	Norma Redo, Mexico	Pre-1571, Mexico	Small skull surmounted by gold cross
Rose Quartz Skull	Rose Quartz	Unknown	Old or Ancient. Central America	Moveable jawbone comparable to M-Hedges
Roseheart	Rose Quartz	Boris Schneickert, Germany	New activated skull. Brazil	3.6kg. Boris is president of IKA
Sam	Quartz	Jaap Van Etten, USA	Brazil. Unique shape. Activated	Weight fluctuates 12-15lbs
San Jose Skull	Amethyst	Unknown	Unknown. Mexico	According to IKA, a very negative skull
Sha Na Ra	Quartz	Nocerino family, USA	Ancient or Old. Guerro, Mexico	13lbs. Excavated 1995
She'Shona	Quartz	Lia Scallon, Australia	Modern, Brazil	3kg. Many rainbows inside
Skully	Quartz	Unknown	Old	Discovered 1997 in auction by David Leslie
Smithsonian	Cloudy Quartz	Smithsonian Inst, USA	Modern or Old, possibly Aztec	Anonymous donation. Hollow. 25.5 cm, 14kg
Synergy	Quartz	Sherry Whitfield	Ancient. Peru or Mu	15.5lbs
Templar Skull	Quartz	French secret society	Unknown	N Nocerino saw this skull during WWII
The Jesuit	Quartz	Joky Van Dieten, Netherlands	Unknown	One-third life size. Connected with Jesuits
The Twins	Nephrite Jade	Kathleen Murray, Scotland	Unknown	Double skull from Mongolian temple
Tibetan Skull	Quartz with ivory eyes	Unknown	Old	Unearthed 1927. Represents Palden Lhamo
Windsong	Quartz	Floyd Petri, USA	1700s. Amazon region	Made by a blind craftsman and shaman
Xa-mu-k'u	Citrine Quartz	Star Johnsen-Moser, USA	Ancient	Used ceremonially in Mayalands
Zar	Opaque white	DaEl Walker, USA	Ancient	Hollow. Neanderthal or hybrid human

APPENDIX FIVE

·

Star Johnsen–Moser's Work
with *Max*

With thanks to Star Johnsen-Moser for inclusion of this material.

Crystal skulls have been used by the ancient ones and continue to be used as an interface between dimensions, assisting intelligent life-forms in inter-dimensional communication. They are also holographic repositories of knowledge.

I will share with you some of my personal experiences with this phenomenon.

During one very powerful group meditation session with *Max*, an ancient Mayan crystal skull, a brilliant pink light began emanating from the skull. By and by we found ourselves being lifted into another dimension wherein we observed a group of beings projecting light through their crystal skull, which was being transmitted inter-dimensionally and received by our group through the crystal skull with which we were working on this dimension. In this experience I felt an intense connection with 'home', and a deep yearning in the knowing that I would have much more to experience on Earth before I could remain evermore in that exquisite, loving energy.

One day, while in the midst of giving healings, I felt a huge power emerge from the depths of my heart and move up into my throat, and suddenly a very strange language burst forth from out of my mouth! I felt totally overpowered by this force and, as I allowed myself to speak, I noticed that the energies of the body of the person on whom I was working seemed to respond to and understand this language. I received the guidance that *Max* the crystal skull would understand this language too!

So I flew to Houston and my friend Mae (who had also begun speaking in the same strange language as myself) and I went to pay *Max* a visit, at the guardian JoAnn Parks' house. As we both allowed ourselves to speak, we noticed that there was some movement in the energies of the skull. They began to quicken enormously and we saw little wheels of light … chakras … begin to whirl within the crystal.

All of a sudden, a presence came flying out of the skull with such force that Mae was literally thrown across the room and landed on the floor. I was frozen to the spot in amazement, the energy was so intense, and every possible emotion was passing through me. Suddenly a laser of light shot from out of the heart centre of this being and shot into my heart, and I thought that my life was suddenly coming to a close, that I was about to literally burst into flames. When I could handle no more, this energy grounded into the earth through my body, and from that moment on I found myself to be in telepathic communion with this presence … whom I call *Tak*.

I continued to be downloaded with this strange language, which I could understand through my emotional body but not with my intellect. However, early on in our relationship I was given the interpretation of *Tak's* mission, which I received while channelling through a Tibetan crystal:

I come to you openly, in Mind and in Heart.

I come to you through the Corridors of Time.

I come to restore your gifts, long forgotten.

I come in remembering, and I come in truth.

I come in Oneness, and I come in gladness.

I come with the blessings of Infinite Love.

Max, JoAnn Parks and I travelled throughout the US for almost three years together, working with groups of lightworkers, both large and small, fulfilling *Tak*'s mission of helping us to remember our Oneness. The climax came during our last activation ceremony. A hologram emerged from the skull and filled the entire room. We found ourselves on top of a pyramid engaged in a Mayan fire ceremony. It felt so real that our eyes burned from the smoke and we could feel the heat from the fire. Suddenly we felt we were being transported totally off the planet and went flying through space ... it felt like we were going through the middle star in Orion's belt. Where we landed we hadn't a clue, for it was so distant that our brains could not bring this information back into this dimension. My work with *Max* the crystal skull was complete. We had fulfilled our purpose together.

·

The Tibetan Crystal Skull *Amar*

Grace of www.crystalskulls.com is the guardian of the rare Tibetan crystal skull, *Amar* – a 22lb quartz skull that was hand-carried across the perilous Himalayan Mountains by a Tibetan Lama in 2005, rescuing it from the Chinese invasion, which has seen over 6,000 monasteries decimated and sacred objects destroyed since the Chinese occupation began in 1950.

Grace has been a crystal healer and internationally acclaimed psychic for 20 years, and has worked extensively with *Amar* since a series of synchronistic events unexpectedly brought this crystal skull to her in early 2006.

The following is a message channelled by Grace from *Amar* in response to the three questions posed by the author during her crystal skull quest. The underlying message throughout this book has been the growth of consciousness – superconsciousness – leading to evolution of *Homo spiritus* through choosing the positive timeline, whilst caring for our planet and her peoples. Others refer to this process as 'ascension', Oneness or enlightenment. Grace's information is included here because it succinctly sums up the role of crystal skulls at this pivotal point in human evolution.

Through *Amar*, Crystal Skull

Crystal skulls are an ancient technology. They were used to access and tap into the Earth's primeval energies and also to access the cosmos. They were used to amplify thought and consciousness. Those who worked with crystal skulls had no other distractions. They worked with them in meditation for days, weeks, months, years, lifetimes. They not only meditated with the crystal skulls, they used them for healing purposes.

The crystal skulls could not only affect the energetic vibration of the body, they could also work with the psyche and consciousness of the individual to restore balance, wellbeing and sanity. This is also true of crystal skulls today. The intention of the practitioner is extremely important. Crystal skulls send out information and receive information. They take everything literally, although they certainly do have a sense of humour!

The role of crystal skulls in ancient times was to be conduits for higher wisdom, knowledge and education for mankind and for those who sought such higher knowledge. Also, as this knowledge was imparted and received, the crystal skulls became receptacles or vessels in which to store this knowledge for future seekers. The crystal skulls are meant to be handed down from generation to generation of shamans, healers, sages and leaders, to guide them in the future, as others have been guided in the past.

Each generation can improve upon the previous generation by benefiting from their knowledge, wisdom and experience. Each subsequent generation adds to this information, enriching all. Crystal skulls are therefore recorders, not only of individual knowledge and experience, but also of human knowledge and experience. They can tap into the energy of anywhere on Earth or in the cosmos, throughout the cosmos, and they are a link, a receiver and a satellite relay system for our space brethren.

Quartz is harmonic and responds to harmonics. Quartz serves to help balance the resonance of humanity and of the Earth. Crystal skulls in materials other than quartz function differently and serve very different purposes. Quartz was the original design, and is, in our opinion, most effective and efficient for computing purposes. We are not relics, we are not artefacts, we are living, breathing consciousness that is frozen in time. We are very much alive, as is the Earth, and we work with the Earth, with humanity, with nature and with the cosmos. We are multidimensional beings – once we are formed into a human skull, we come alive. We gain life-force and consciousness that is far greater than simple crystalline consciousness.

The crystal skull transcends time and space, transcends form and function. It helps to elevate mankind, both physically and consciously. Quartz skulls and other crystal skulls raise the frequency of the human body and restore balance and wellbeing. Once balance is restored, enough of mankind's incessant and perpetual lunacy can be overcome so that the individual and those around him or her can then attune to higher frequencies of consciousness. The crystal skulls are now multiplying in force to assure several things: the ascension of the Earth and the ascension of mankind. We hold the frequency of the planet in check so it can maintain its equilibrium even as mankind's insanity threatens to blow the Earth to kingdom come.

The crystal skulls are connected to each other through the crystal skulls grid, much like a cosmic internet surrounding your planet. We can exchange energy and information with other crystal skulls anywhere in the world – those that have surfaced as well as those that remain hidden. We do not have to be in direct proximity to other crystal skulls in order to have this energy-transference or this exchange of information. We do indeed have a mind of our own.

New skulls are not activated, not turned on or programmed. Older skulls activate and program these neophyte skulls in order to awaken all those around them and to restore balance throughout their environment, and indeed, throughout the world. Crystal skulls can also communicate with other crystalline beings, and with the crystalline consciousness within all things. We can restore order and balance wherever we are.

We can also create chaos and amplify that chaos, if we are misused. It is like static on a television when an antenna is knocked out. We can create a great deal of static when used in the wrong hands or in the wrong way. This is why shamans and spiritual practitioners were taught and schooled for many years on the right use of crystal skulls. Crystal skulls became sought and prized for their power and their ability to amplify power, thought and intention, but whatever energy one puts out gets amplified by a crystal skull a thousandfold. Beware.

The connection between the Maya crystal skulls, or the crystal skulls from the Americas and those in the Himalayas, is powerful and ancient, but it is a story that most people are not ready to believe. Crystal skulls were scattered to the four corners of the Earth, partly to mitigate wanton misuse of their power, and partly to anchor the energies of the Earth to preserve her wellbeing.

There are crystal skulls on all known and unknown continents. There are many crystal skulls that have yet to be discovered. There are many more than thirteen original crystal skulls, but there are crystal skulls given or forged by each of the ancient tribes on Earth on continents and in places that no longer exist – many of these were moved and transported to the Americas and to the Himalayas for safekeeping until the time of the ascension arose. That time is now.

Not all of the crystal skulls need to surface, nor will they. Some must remain buried in order to anchor certain energies vitally in the Earth. Some crystal skulls must surface in order to raise consciousness and bring their knowledge and wisdom to those around them. Some crystal skulls have been shut down or turned off, and need to be reactivated, but this will come in time as the quickening continues.

With thanks to Grace and www.crystalskulls.com *for inclusion of this transmission.*

·

Practical Considerations

Innerscape-ability

This is an example of how to develop innerscape-ability using either a picture of a crystal skull (on internet is best, because the skull is then interacting with crystal technology and light) or, if you are fortunate, a real one.

Focus with a soft kind of gaze upon the crystal skull. Breathe in and out effortlessly through your nose, relaxing your body. If you sense you are holding onto difficult emotions or mental stress concentrate on your *out-going* breath, making your exhalation twice as long as your inhalation (you can check this by counting). It might sound like a big sigh! Continue until you feel you have nothing left to release, feeling warmth at your physical and spiritual heart.

Re-focus upon the crystal skull. From now on, breathe softly and deeply. Take a quick check around your body to ensure it feels soft and relaxed: feet, legs, hips, abdomen, chest, back, arms, hands, neck, face, head, outside and inside your skull.

Now *close your eyes* and recall the sacred pyramid within your skull. Mentally draw a silver line from between your eyebrows (the brow or *ajna* chakra), to the base of the skull at the back of the neck (the *alta major* chakra). Join this silver line to the very centre of the top of your skull (the Crown or *sahasrara* chakra) then take this line down between your eyebrows. You have drawn a silver triangle or pyramid. Within the very centre of this pyramid sits pure consciousness, pure being.

Actually it is a void, but at this moment if you wish to visualize further then see this part of your innerscape as a golden sphere. This sphere is as large or as small as you wish to make it; it can stay within your head, serve as a psychic protection around your body, or be expanded to encompass the globe of the Earth. Now the sphere is so light that it can float out of your skull into the very centre of the crystal skull. There it melds, merges, transforms, becoming part of that individual skull's heritage and potential, before coming back to centre in your own skull.

Let the golden sphere settle within. Absorb whatever it has to convey to you. Know that you have connected with superconsciousness and have ridden the wave of Time-Spirit.

Ceremony and Release of Karma

When ceremony is intensely engaged upon with good intention, essences are released which open participants to worlds beyond the visible, other-dimensional realities, the quantum field and particularly the part of it which comprises superconsciousness and Time-Spirit. Ceremony doesn't have to be strange or shamanic in nature. It doesn't even have to be religious or spiritual to move us into deep levels of perception.

A simple ceremony can be ritualistically devised by anyone. All you need is a positive meaningful intention. Components of ceremony can be:

- special words, prayers or a poem; offerings of flowers, food or candles;

- a photograph of a loved one or a picture of a divine being;

- a crystal skull or a pattern or 'layout' in crystal healing terms, of a number of crystals or twelve small crystal skulls in a circle;

- a circle or 'medicine wheel' (meaning a representation of good intention) marked upon the ground and orientated with markers to the four compass points. This forms the earthly matrix which interfaces with natural laws and nurtures ceremony in a sacred space.

Note that when engaging in ceremonies, 'calling in' the ancestors and keepers of the directions to assist us, especially if occurring within a medicine wheel, immediately shifts our perceptions.

To specifically release karma, call upon the force of grace which, if invoked in truth and good intention, can only comply with the request. This release is most powerful in the presence of two friends – one to witness, one the 'reader' to read the words, slowly, for you to repeat. However, it can be done on your own but the words *must always be read slowly out loud* with conviction.

To proceed, place a chair before an open window or, ideally, sit outside in a quiet natural place. Your friends stand one on each side and slightly behind you. (The release that liberates you from *karma* works through your physical, emotional, mental and spiritual bodies. It is cathartic, so you don't want a person standing in front of you to take on any negativity!)

The 'reader' begins, saying the words, line by line, for the recipient to speak clearly out loud:

Superconsciousness, by the force of grace,
I formally rescind all ties and attachments
to Earth-bound *karma* and dark forces
entered into in this or any other lifetime.
So that the power of that release
Is fully manifest in my consciousness.
(Deep releasing out-breath by the recipient.)
And so it is.

Bibliography

Friedel, David, Schele, Linda and Parker, Joy, *Maya Comos*, William Morrow, 1993

Laszlo, Ervin, *The Akashic Experience*, Inner Traditions, 2009

Laszlo, Ervin, *Quantum Shift in the Global Brain*, Inner Traditions, 2008

McTaggart, Lynne, *The Field*, Harper Collins, 2001

Men, Hunbatz, *The Eight Calendars of the Maya*, Bear & Co, 2010

Mercier, Patricia, *The Maya Shamans – Travellers in Time*, Vega, 2002

Mercier, Patricia, *The Maya End Times*, Watkins, 2008

Morton, C & Thomas, C L, *The Mystery of the Crystal Skulls*, Thorsons, 1997

Schele, L & Freidel, D, *A Forest of Kings*, William Morrow, 1990

Acknowledgements and Contacts

I wish to thank all of the crystal skulls and guardians that have contributed in many ways to this book. In addition a special mention for the support of friends including the Dreamtime Kin, Elmera and my husband Mikhail. Grateful thanks to Professor Ervin Laszlo (www.clubofbudapest.org and www.giordanobrunouniversity. com) and Dr Carl Calleman (www.calleman.com) for use of quotations. Plus all of the following:

Joseph Bennett www.atlanteanskull.com
www.crystalskull-compassion.com

Alice Friend www.alicefriend.com

Grace www.crystalskulls.com

Hunbatz Men, Itzá Maya tradition www.themayas.com.mx

Star Johnsen-Moser www.ponyexpress.net

LionFire Shaman http://people.tribe.net/lionfireshaman
http://www.livetolovetolive.com/LionFire.html
www.myspace.com/lionfireshaman

Kendal Ray Morgan   www.crystalskullsevents.com

Kathleen Murray and Gillian Ellis   www.crystal-keys.com www.crystals.eu.com

Don Alejandro Cirilo Perez Oxlaj   www.shiftingages.com

Dr Rock, Maya calendar converter   www.dr-rock.biz

Lia Scallon   www.soundsofsirius.com

Boris Schneickert   www.ika-international.org

Joshua Shapiro   www.v-j-enterprises.com

Shavaty   www.crystalunity.com

Lydia Trauttenberg
www.crystalskulls.com/lydia-trauttenberg.html

DaEl and Laurie Walker   www.crystalawareness.com

Sherry Whitfield   www.crystal-skull.com

Joanne van Wijgerden   www.healingarts.nl